W9-DCU-871

Billy Graham

Also by Deborah Hart Strober and Gerald S. Strober

Let Us Begin Anew: An Oral History of the
Kennedy Presidency

Nixon: An Oral History of His Presidency

Reagan: The Man and His Presidency

The Monarchy: An Oral Biography of Elizabeth II

His Holiness the Dalai Lama: The Oral Biography

BILLY GRAHAM

AN ORAL AND NARRATIVE BIOGRAPHY

Deborah Hart Strober and Gerald S. Strober

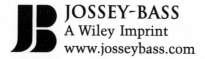

JOSSEY-BASS
A Wiley Imprint
www.josseybass.com

Published by Jossey-Bass
A Wiley Imprint
989 Market Street, San Francisco, CA 94103-1741   www.josseybass.com

Jossey-Bass books and products are available through most bookstores. To contact Jossey-Bass directly call our Customer Care Department within the U.S. at 800-956-7739, outside the U.S. at 317-572-3986, or fax 317-572-4002.

Jossey-Bass also publishes its books in a variety of electronic formats. Some content that appears in print may not be available in electronic books.

Library of Congress Cataloging-in-Publication Data
Strober, Deborah H. (Deborah Hart), date.
Billy Graham: an oral and narrative biography / Deborah Hart Strober and Gerald S. Strober.
p. cm.
Includes bibliographical references and index.
ISBN-13: 978–0–7879–8401–4 (cloth)
ISBN-10: 0–7879–8401–9 (cloth)
1. Graham, Billy, 1918- .   2. Evangelists—United States—Biography.
I. Strober, Gerald S.   II. Title.
BV3785.G69S77 2006
269'.2092—dc22
[B]
2006011517

Printed in the United States of America
FIRST EDITION

HB Printing   10 9 8 7 6 5 4 3 2 1

CONTENTS

Illustrations follow page 74

To our grandchildren

Eyal Jonathan Benjamin
Ran Michael Benjamin
Kai Wesley Philip Sterling
Marley Grace Sterling

PREFACE

Following our marriage in 1981, we decided to collaborate on compiling oral histories and biographies of notable personalities, among them three U.S. presidents, Queen Elizabeth II, the Fourteenth Dalai Lama, and Rudolf Giuliani. During the spring of 2005, mindful that Mr. Graham's New York City Crusade, which would take place in June, was likely to be the evangelist's last, we decided to chronicle his amazing life and works in *Billy Graham: An Oral and Narrative Biography.*

Over the years, we have encountered the famed evangelist both in social settings and at crusades, most recently in Cincinnati in 2003. As Gerald recalls the initial encounter:

> I first met Billy Graham in the spring of 1956 while attending his Richmond, Virginia, Crusade just a few weeks before I entered the army on May 18. I could never have imagined that that first and brief encounter would be followed, years later, by meetings both at his home and in a number of cities where he held crusades. Nor could I then have known that I would write three books on aspects of his life and ministry. Or that I would come to serve as an unofficial intermediary between him and the government of Israel. And I could never have imagined that I would in time come to know the physically and spiritually imposing "Mr. Graham" as "Billy."

All of that was well in the future when, at the kind intervention of a major in the Salvation Army, I was introduced to Billy one evening following his sermon and invitation. I was nervous at the prospect of coming face-to-face with him; he was the first famous person I had ever met, and to say that I had little in common with the evangelist—then on the cusp of the world fame that would come his way a year later in Madison Square Garden—was more than an understatement.

I had been listening to his Sunday night *Hour of Decision* broadcast since I was nineteen and a student at Brooklyn College. In those years— the heart of the cold war—Billy preached a strident anticommunism, but I was more interested in what he had to say about personal salvation and my need for a relationship with Christ. It was a combination of his preaching, my own nascent study of the Bible, and the ministrations of the Reverend Lockerbie of the Bay Ridge Baptist Church that led me (Brooklyn-born, -bred, and Jewish) to accept Christ as Lord and Savior. This difficult path began, innocently enough, outside the gates of Brooklyn College when a well-dressed man in his twenties handed me a pocket-sized copy of the New Testament. Two decades later, I would return to the Jewish community. But that is a story for another time.

The Richmond Crusade was taking place in a football stadium, a setting similar to that of many of Billy's other large gatherings. As I sat in the bleachers waiting for the Salvation Army major to take me to meet the up-and-coming evangelist, I wondered what to say. My life's experiences were quite limited; other than this trip to Virginia's capital, I had hardly been out of New York City. The U.S. Army would soon remedy that situation, however, posting me first to Fort Sill, Oklahoma, and then to West Germany.

Now the moment of our meeting was at hand. The Salvation Army major said to Billy, "I would like to introduce you to this Jewish young man who has come here from New York." The evangelist asked my name, warmly shook my hand, and said, "God bless you." Several seconds later, someone else attracted his attention and Billy turned to greet that person. I was not at all disappointed at the brevity of my encounter with him, however. I had actually stood next to Billy, shaken his hand, and experienced the impact of the gaze of his penetrating blue eyes. My trip to Richmond was more than worthwhile.

We trust that readers of *Billy Graham: An Oral and Narrative Biography* will share our appreciation of this modest yet forceful man from North Carolina who traveled the world in the name of his Lord.

Deborah Hart Strober
Gerald S. Strober
New York, May 2006

BIBLIOGRAPHIC NOTE

Writing this book was facilitated by our reference to Billy Graham's auto-biography, *Just As I Am* (HarperSanFrancisco, 1997); William Martin's authorized biography, *A Prophet with Honor: The Billy Graham Story* (William Morrow, 1991); Curtis Mitchell's *God in the Garden: The Story of the Billy Graham New York Crusade* (Doubleday, 1957); Lowell D. Streiker and Gerald S. Strober's *Religion and the New Majority: Billy Graham, Middle America and the Politics of the '70s* (Association Press, 1972); our own book, *A Day in the Life of Billy Graham* (Square One Pub-lishers, 2003); and interviews we conducted over more than thirty years. In addition, we referred to press releases and other publications issued by the Billy Graham Evangelistic Association.

ACKNOWLEDGMENTS

We could not have compiled *Billy Graham: An Oral and Narrative Biography* without the gracious cooperation and encouragement of our interviewees, many of them long-time associates of Mr. Graham's. We also want to express our appreciation to A. Larry Ross, the evangelist's able media representative; his efficient assistant, Melany Ethridge; Mark DeMoss, Franklin Graham's representative and a friend of long standing; and Erik Ogren of the Billy Graham Evangelistic Association, all of whom responded promptly, and most helpfully, to our requests for information and other assistance.

We deeply appreciate the efforts of Hana Lane, the editor at John Wiley & Sons of our oral histories of the Dalai Lama and Rudolph Giuliani—the latter to be published in January 2007—in encouraging us to chronicle the life of Billy Graham and for bringing our idea to the attention of Jossey-Bass, a Wiley imprint.

At Jossey-Bass, we appreciate the editing skills, not to mention the encouragement and anticipation, of executive editor Sheryl Fullerton, who spoke of how she was "looking forward to the adventures of creating this new book." We also want to thank Catherine Craddock, assistant editor of Jossey-Bass's Religion and Spirituality Series, Andrea Flint, Sandy Siegle, and Thomas Finnegan for their assistance.

As with our six other oral biographies to date, we could not have made it through our many months of interviewing, writing, and polishing a manuscript without the love and encouragement of our close and devoted friends, siblings, children and their partners, and our four remarkable grandchildren.

CHRONOLOGY

November 17, 1918	William Frank Graham, Jr., is born on a farm in Charlotte, North Carolina
June 10, 1920	Ruth McCue Bell (the future Mrs. Billy Graham) is born in Qingjiang, China
1934	Billy Graham makes personal commitment to Christ
1936	Enrolls in Bob Jones College, Cleveland, Tennessee
1937	Transfers to Florida Bible Institute, near Tampa
1939	Is ordained as a Southern Baptist minister
1940	Graduates from Florida Bible Institute and enrolls at Wheaton College, Wheaton, Illinois
August 13, 1943	Marries Ruth Bell, his Wheaton schoolmate, in Montreat, North Carolina
1943	Graduates from Wheaton and becomes pastor of nearby Western Springs Baptist Church
1945	Joins Youth for Christ as the organization's first full-time employee
1945	Ruth gives birth to their first child, Virginia, followed by births of Anne Morrow (1948), Ruth (1950), Franklin (1952), and Nelson (1958)
1945–1947	Billy travels throughout the United States and Europe for Youth for Christ

1948	Is appointed president of Northwestern Schools, Minneapolis
1949	Is catapulted to fame after conducting an eight-week tent meeting in downtown Los Angeles
1950	Makes first broadcast of "The Hour of Decision" radio program
1950	Meets with President Harry S. Truman in the first of many sessions with presidents through George W. Bush
1950	Establishment of the Billy Graham Evangelistic Association (BGEA)
1952	Billy resigns as Northwestern Schools' president to conduct citywide evangelistic meetings
1953	Writes *Peace with God,* the first of more than a score of best-selling books
1954	Holds twelve-week Crusade at Harringay Arena, London
1956	Publication of first issue of *Christianity Today*
1957	Billy holds sixteen-week Crusade in Madison Square Garden
1959	Conducts four-month tour of Australia
1960–2005	Holds hundreds of crusades throughout the United States and the world
1973	Preaches to 1.1 million people at final service of Crusade in Seoul, Korea
1974	First International Congress on Evangelism is held in Lausanne, Switzerland
1984	Billy preaches in the Soviet Union; returns in 1988 and 1992
1988	Makes first visit to the People's Republic of China; returns in 1992 and 1994

1992	Makes first visit to North Korea; returns in 1994
April 23, 1995	Addresses Memorial Prayer Service for victims of Oklahoma City bombing
1996	With Ruth, receives Congressional Gold Medal
September 14, 2001	Addresses National Day of Prayer and Remembrance for victims of attacks on September 11
2002	Breaks attendance record at Riverfront Stadium, Cincinnati, Ohio
2002	Breaks attendance record at Texas Stadium, Irving
2004	Holds Crusade in Rose Bowl, Pasadena, California
June 24–26, 2005	Holds final Crusade in Corona Park, Queens, New York

THE INTERVIEWEES

The Reverend Lane Adams is a former associate evangelist with the Billy Graham Evangelistic Association (BGEA). He was interviewed on January 11, 2005, by telephone.

Lois K. Akehurst is the wife of Rev. William Akehurst, the regional center chairman of the Baltimore, Maryland, center of the BGEA's TV Telephone Ministry. Mrs. Akehurst attended Mr. Graham's Madison Square Garden Crusade in 1957. Coming full circle in the evangelist's forty-eight-year mission to New York, she was interviewed on the evening of June 24, 2005, during the opening session of the New York Crusade in Corona Park, Queens.

Ben Armstrong, the former executive vice president of the National Religious Broadcasters, has been a friend to Billy Graham since the 1940s. He was interviewed on December 12, 2005, by telephone.

Arthur Bailey, a long-time member of Mr. Graham's ministry, serves as crusade associate of the BGEA. He was the director of the New York Crusade at Corona Park, Queens, in 2005. Following Mr. Graham's last crusade, Mr. Bailey went on to Baltimore, Maryland, to oversee Franklin Graham's major Festival there. He was interviewed on August 23, 2005, at the New York Crusade's office in New York City.

Gerald Beavan is a long-time associate of Billy Graham's. He served as a professor and registrar of the Northwestern Schools, located in Minneapolis, Minnesota. He was interviewed on December 9, 2005, by telephone.

Bill Brown is the husband of Joan Winmill Brown. He is the former president of World Wide Pictures and a member of the BGEA. He was interviewed on December 30, 2005, by telephone.

Joan Winmill Brown is the wife of Bill Brown. An actress and author, she was counseled by Ruth Graham at Billy Graham's London Crusade in 1954. She was interviewed on December 30, 2005, by telephone.

Dwight Chapin was recruited in 1967 by Richard M. Nixon for his first successful presidential campaign and then served during his administration as appointments secretary. He was interviewed on December 27, 2005, by telephone.

Michael Deaver, a longtime associate of Ronald W. Reagan's, served as the deputy chief of staff during Mr. Reagan's presidency. He was interviewed on December 28, 2005, by telephone.

Millie Dienert, prayer coordinator of the Billy Graham crusades, is the wife of the late Fred Dienert, a partner in the Walter Bennett Agency. The Dienerts and the Grahams were very close friends. She was interviewed on December 21, 2005, by telephone.

The Reverend David Epstein, senior pastor of the Calvary Baptist Church, served as a member of the executive committee of the Billy Graham New York Crusade in 2005. He was interviewed on September 20, 2005, at the church's offices on West 57th Street in New York City.

Rev. Paul Ferrin is the son of the late Dr. Howard Ferrin, the former president of the Providence Bible Institute, later Barrington College, located in Rhode Island. Howard Ferrin was involved in Billy Graham's Boston and New England Crusades in 1950 and 1951, respectively. His son was interviewed on December 7, 2005, by telephone.

Helen Stam Fesmire was a housemate of Ruth Bell Graham's at Wheaton College, in Illinois, were she met both her future husband, the Reverend Lloyd Fesmire, and his fellow student, friend, and ministerial colleague, Billy Graham. She was interviewed on December 2, 2005, by telephone.

The Reverend Leighton Ford, a brother-in-law of Billy Graham's (he is the husband of Mr. Graham's sister Jean), is a former associate evangelist with the BGEA. He was interviewed on January 16, 2006, by telephone.

The Reverend Henry Holley serves as the BGEA's director of Asian affairs and in that capacity accompanied Mr. Graham on his visits to China and North Korea. He was interviewed on January 6, 2006, by telephone.

The Reverend Robert J. Johannson is the senior pastor of the Evangel Church, located in Long Island City, New York. He served as pastoral chairman and member of the 2005 New York Crusade Committee. He was interviewed on September 21, 2005, at his offices at the church.

The Reverend Howard O. Jones, now retired, served as an associate evangelist with the BGEA for many years. He was interviewed on December 6, 2005, by telephone.

The Reverend Dr. Dale Kietzman was a schoolmate of Billy Graham's at Wheaton College. He is currently a professor at the William Carey International University in Pasadena, California. He recommended to the North Korean ambassador to the United Nations that Mr. Graham be invited to North Korea. He was interviewed on December 22, 2005, by telephone.

The Reverend Billy Kim is president of the Far East Broadcasting Company and a former president of the Baptist World Alliance. He served as the interpreter for Billy Graham during the 1973 Crusade in Seoul, South Korea. He was interviewed on November 9, 2005, by telephone.

Dr. Dwight Linton, for twenty-five years a missionary in Korea, was recruited by his nephew, Stephen Linton, to serve as an interpreter to Billy Graham on the evangelist's first visit to North Korea in 1992. He was interviewed on December 28, 2005, by telephone.

Stephen Linton is chairman of the Eugene Bell Foundation. He served as a consultant to and interpreter for Billy Graham on the evangelist's visits to North Korea in 1992 and 1994, having recruited his uncle, Dr. Dwight Linton, to serve with him on the first visit. He was interviewed on December 20, 2005, by telephone.

Betty Bao Lord, an author and human rights activist, is the wife of Winston Lord, the U.S. ambassador to the People's Republic of China during Billy and Ruth Graham's first visit to that nation. She was interviewed on December 21, 2005, by telephone.

Winston Lord was the U.S. ambassador to the People's Republic of China during Billy and Ruth Graham's first visit to that nation and is the husband of Betty Bao Lord. He was interviewed on December 21, 2005, by telephone.

Anna-Lisa Madeira, née Beckman, a classmate of Ruth Bell and Billy Graham's at Wheaton College, was the founder and a member of Carolers for Christ, the quartet that performed on the "Songs in the Night" radio program. Hired to assist Mr. Graham in his office, she was likely his first secretary. She was interviewed on December 13, 2005, by telephone.

William Martin is the Harry and Hazel Chavanne Professor of Religion and Public Policy at Rice University, in Houston, Texas, where he serves as chairman of the Department of Sociology. A prolific writer, he is the authorized biographer of Billy Graham. He was interviewed on the evening of June 24, 2005, during the opening session of the New York Crusade in Corona Park, Queens.

Rev. Charles Massey was a classmate of Billy Graham's at the Florida Bible Institute. He went on to serve as a chaplain in the U.S. Army and is now retired. He was interviewed on December 6, 2005, by telephone.

Joyce Mostrom, née Ferrin, is the daughter of Dr. Howard Ferrin, the late president of the Providence Bible Institute. She and her future husband, Don Mostrom, were classmates of Ruth Bell and Billy Graham's at Wheaton College. Mrs. Mostrom also sang in Carolers for Christ. She was interviewed on December 12, 2005, by telephone.

Roger Palms has served as the assistant editor, associate editor, and editor of *Decision* magazine, the official publication of the BGEA. He was interviewed on December 6, 2005, by telephone.

Charles Riggs, a former crusade director for the BGEA, has known Mr. Graham since the late 1940s. He was interviewed on December 15, 2005, by telephone.

Sidney Rittenberg, an academician and business consultant, formerly resided in the People's Republic of China, where he was imprisoned for sixteen years. He went on to serve as Billy Graham's interpreter on his visits to China in 1988, 1992, and 1994. He was interviewed on December 5, 2005, by telephone.

Maurice Rowlandson formerly served as director of the BGEA office in London. He was interviewed on December 5, 2005, by telephone.

Louis Zamperini, a former University of Southern California track star and member of the U.S. track team at the 1936 Olympic Games, was converted at Billy Graham's Los Angeles meeting in 1949. He was interviewed on December 15, 2005, by telephone.

Billy Graham

Chapter One

NEW YORK, 2005

The Press Conference

It is shortly before noon on Tuesday, June 21, 2005. His once golden—and now white—mane reaching almost to his collar and combed back to accentuate his etched-in-granite profile, Billy Graham enters a crowded suite adjacent to Rockefeller Center's fabled Rainbow Room on this hot and sunny morning, to a barrage of whirring cameras and deferential murmurs from New York's usually blasé press corps.

The Reverend Robert J. Johannson, senior pastor, Evangel Church, Long Island City, New York; pastoral chairman, member, 2005 New York Crusade Committee   Dr. Graham said to us, "We will get a good press in New York." That's the genius of the Graham people; there is not a person in New York City who did not know he was there. No one else has that kind of clout. We, who have been marginalized in the media, have been put on their radar because of the Graham meeting. For that, it was worth all the effort. The Graham crusade took us who were marginalized and said: "Hey, we are here all the time. Come see what we are doing."

Rev. David Epstein, senior pastor, Calvary Baptist Church, New York City; member, Executive Committee, 2005 Billy Graham New York Crusade   I was so amazed and appreciative of the way the press treated him. The Gospel got such positive reception. As I told my congregation, even the *New York Times* preached the Gospel that week!

Using a walker, Graham haltingly makes his way to a dais set up in the center of the large rectangular room and eases his massive, but now weary, body into a chair. He appears tired, his face betraying the strains of his numerous illnesses and recent accidents.

Arthur Bailey, crusade associate, Billy Graham Evangelistic Association (BGEA); director, New York Crusade, Corona Park, Queens, 2005   A group in New York City wanted Mr. Graham to conduct a crusade closely following September 11. Mr. Graham felt that this might appear too opportunistic and declined. There was an open invitation to come to New York, but Billy couldn't commit since he was not certain he could fulfill such an obligation. The group began meeting in December 2003, and by the fall of 2004 a formal invitation was extended. Mr. Graham gave the go-ahead, and we opened an office in Manhattan with the goal of holding a crusade in Central Park in June 2005. In April, I arranged for a group of pastors on the crusade committee to meet with Mr. Graham at his office in Black Mountain, North Carolina. The very morning they were to fly down—they were at the airport—I received a call from Mr. Graham's assistant, David Bruce, saying that Billy had fallen for the second time that year and fractured his pelvis. So the meeting was cancelled.

Robert J. Johannson   We wanted to do something special to honor him because New York might be his last crusade. Those of us from a charismatic background believe that a pastor could pass on a blessing, like Elijah's mantle. We thought, Let's have a special meeting in Madison Square Garden and then a mass meeting in Central Park. We will make the Garden meeting like George Washington's Farewell Address to the troops. He will come; he will pray for us; he will ask God to use us in evangelism. There were people scheduled to attend from the West Coast, from London, and from Africa for this final blessing of Dr. Graham's ministry. But Dr. Graham is an old Southern Baptist, and I don't think he understood our charismatic aspect. So I think his response to our plan was, "I'm an evangelist, I want to preach the Gospel." So the whole idea was put off. I was amazed at his marvelous focus.

The Graham people came to us a long time ago. I was at the first meeting held at the Marriott Hotel, in Manhattan. In almost every instance where Dr. Graham has gone in his ministry, he was very seriously sought after and invited. As Dr. Graham saw the curtain coming down (so to speak), he recalled some of his greatest crusades—New York City, Kansas City, Los Angeles—and, as it was told to me, he wanted to go to those three cities. So his people came to us and asked if we would consider inviting him. And we replied, "Of course." So this Crusade came out of the heart of Billy Graham.

The room quiets. The cameras cease their annoying whir. Mr. Graham, as he prefers to be called, eschewing the more formal "Reverend Graham," is introduced by Larry Ross, his communications officer. Suddenly, the eighty-seven-year-old legend is transformed. His color rising, he quips, "I've never seen so many cameras except for when I got back from a peace conference in Moscow because they wanted to criticize me."

Ben Armstrong, former executive vice president, National Religious Broadcasters; friend to Graham since the 1940s I moderated the press conference he held in New York upon his return from Moscow in 1982. He was embattled because of reports that he had gone into forbidden territory. Our government was not too happy about it; people from the right were not too happy. He had to face up to all of this in the press conference.

The evangelist notes his long relationship with the American Jewish community—and particularly his friendship with the late Rabbi Marc Tanenbaum of the American Jewish Committee—and says, "I look forward to meeting with some of them."

Then, shifting gears, Graham deals with the issue of his own mortality with both gravity and humor, in the first instance recalling that following brain surgery several years earlier "I thought I was dying and all my sins came in front of me" and that he would "welcome death"; and then, addressing the media once again, and particularly the still photographers and television crews, quipping amid much laughter, "I hope I meet all of you there [in heaven], and bring your camera."

Before taking questions, Graham says: "I've loved New York for years, and when I see those signs 'I ♥ NY,' I pray for New York. Thank you for your participation, and God bless you all."

Now Graham, who on entering the room appeared tired and frail, is animated and welcomes questions on a variety of subjects. Reminding the media that he ministered to a congregation for three years early in his career, he says, "I'd love to be a pastor again because I consider myself a pastor." As to whether he would accept an invitation to hold a crusade in London (which he would eventually decline), he leaves the door open, saying, "We're praying about that. This [the New York Crusade] will be our last in America, I'm sure, and we're praying about that." As to the greatest challenges confronting humankind, he opines that "the greatest problem we have is poverty." Asked what his favorite prayer is, he at first ripostes, "I don't have a favorite prayer" but then contradicts himself, saying, "'Lord Help Me' is my favorite prayer."

Arthur Bailey   In a sense, we had been holding the "last" crusade for several years. We thought Jacksonville, in 2000, would be the last. Then there came a number of other crusades, including Fresno, Oklahoma City, Cincinnati, and Dallas. In 2004, Mr. Graham held crusades in Kansas City and Los Angeles. As his health seemed to improve, or at least stabilize, New York came more and more into the picture.

Helen Stam Fesmire, housemate of Ruth Bell Graham, Wheaton College; wife of Rev. Lloyd Fesmire, a friend and colleague of Billy Graham's   My husband had Alzheimer's. Our daughter, who lives in Chicago, read an article to him that said that New York would probably be Billy's last crusade and "Bev" (George Beverly) Shea's last time to sing "How Great Thou Art." In some of the last words he said to us that made sense, my husband responded, "Who *says* it's their last?"

Maurice Rowlandson, former director of BGEA Office, London   Two of us from England—Prebendary Richard Bews, formerly of All Souls Church, Langham Place, and I—were invited to attend the New York Crusade. Unbeknownst to us, Billy wanted to consult us on the possibility of coming back to London. I have to say it was our united advice that it was not the right time to come. First, he was to come in November, and there wasn't enough time to do the proper organization. Second, there wasn't any suitable venue available. But perhaps most important, the London BGEA office was closed in 1987 and since then no records had been maintained, so we had no database to work on.

Arthur Bailey   That decision was made by Mr. Graham and his family. I know that he was very concerned about being away from Mrs. Graham. It was one thing to be in New York, where he could be home in a matter of a few hours, but another thing to be in London. My own thought is that this [the New York Crusade] turned out so well—he did so well—that anything you would do after this would not be as effective. This left him at a level of going out in an appropriate way. So why take the risk of doing anything else that could take the luster away from his success in New York?

Millie Dienert, prayer coordinator, Billy Graham crusades; wife of the late Fred Dienert, partner, Walter Bennett Agency   It was very difficult for him to realize that this was the last time he would preach to a large audience. There was a pull in his heart as he realized it. Also, his was a very grateful heart for the many years the Lord had given him, for the way that God had blessed his ministry. It was a combination: a heart full of gratitude and a heart full of sadness at the same time.

Planning for the 2005 Crusade: Why Not Madison Square Garden?

Arthur Bailey   When we first discussed coming back to New York, Madison Square Garden seemed to be a sentimental choice, but it was just too small a venue. Its capacity of twenty-four thousand could not accommodate the anticipated audience. The committee thought that our mission could best be accomplished by holding a two-day crusade in Central Park, as we had in 1991. In February 2005, when Mr. Graham realized we were getting a huge response from the local churches, he decided that we should look for an outdoor venue. We soon discovered that the city was in the process of rewriting rules for use of the park, and that we would have to hold the Crusade in a fenced-in area within the Sheep Meadow with attendance limited to fifty thousand ticket holders. We concluded that this would not be sufficient, and so we began to look at other possible venues. We found that Yankee Stadium was not available on the dates we wanted. We then met with officials of the New York Mets concerning Shea Stadium. Here the problem involved our need to use the infield to accommodate an expected overflow. The Mets had a game scheduled for two days after the Crusade and their groundskeepers did not believe that they could get the field in shape in such a short period of time.

Robert J. Johannson   Not only didn't we know a few weeks before the meeting where it would be located, we didn't even know if Dr. Graham would be there. In the late spring, I had traveled, along with two other pastors, to North Carolina to meet him. When we entered his house, I thought I was visiting a nursing home; I sat across from Dr. Graham and thought I was looking at death warmed over. Yet as we talked and prayed together, I felt he was going to do it. I thought: here I am, praying for this icon, but he is just a man—a man that God can use.

Seeking to Resolve the Issue of Venue: Cliffhangers and Faith

Arthur Bailey   We had never been in a situation where sixty days out a venue had not been selected, yet we did not panic. I kept telling Mr. Graham that God was sharing Amos 6:8 with me: "I will deliver up the city with all that is therein." We went back to the Mets and agreed on a date one week earlier than originally planned. But then the police informed us that another event was scheduled for Flushing Meadow— the area adjacent to Shea Stadium—for that weekend and that they could not handle two major events on the same day. It seemed that God kept closing doors, leading us, I believe, to the place where He wanted us to have this meeting.

The Thirty-Day Miracle

Arthur Bailey   When we decided to come back to New York, our intention was to make this a crusade to the world. I sent a technical crew out to Flushing Meadow, and as they walked past the Unisphere [a structure that had been erected for the 1964 World's Fair] they came upon a very large open area and someone asked, "Why don't you hold it here?" I went out to look at the site the next day, but I thought it was very rough. I told the crew that we could hold the Crusade there only if we could set up chairs; I was told that, indeed, the area would accommodate seventy thousand chairs.

As we considered the possibility of Flushing Meadow, we were informed that 130 languages were represented in that area. We could not travel to every place in the world, but at Corona Park Mr. Graham would be speaking to the world. If you hold a meeting in Manhattan, you have a more media-based dynamic. If you hold a meeting in Queens, you have an international, people-oriented dynamic. So about thirty days out, we made the decision to go to Flushing Meadow. We called it "The Thirty Day Miracle."

Wednesday, June 22

Arthur Bailey   We took Billy out to Corona Park and rode around in a golf cart. At one point he spent about thirty minutes with a group of Korean pastors who were involved in the Crusade, and he posed for photos with them and thanked them for their help. He didn't comment about the venue, which was still not ready—there were no chairs or tents set up. He never complained. He felt it was a wonderful venue because so many kinds of people, representing so many cultures and languages, would attend.

David Epstein   Art Bailey had great vision. There was some concern but at the same time the conviction that this was the place to be. The Graham organization's experience in dealing with these issues really paid off when you think of the attendance of 200,000 over three days. We could never have achieved that in Central Park because of the limits placed on attendance there.

Corona Park: Friday, June 24–Sunday, June 26, 2005

Friday

On most late Friday afternoons in summer, traffic flows away from Manhattan, the hub of finance and industry, the workplace and entertainment center that is a magnet to millions of residents of the tristate area—suburban New York, New Jersey, and Connecticut. On this afternoon, however, the traffic pattern is quite different: all manner of vehicles are converging on Manhattan and then heading across the bridges and the one tunnel that link the fabled borough with its neighbor to the east, Queens. Their destination at the end of this hot and sunny workweek is Corona Park, the site of what has been billed as likely the Reverend Billy Graham's last Crusade in the United States, and possibly in the world.

For many other crusade attendees who do not own cars, or choose not to drive, or do not wish to take the subway, the journey to Corona Park begins at Manhattan's Pennsylvania Station. It is rush hour, yet thousands—many clutching picnic baskets and guiding small children in strollers—wait patiently in line to purchase tickets for specially arranged Long Island Railroad trains that will whisk them to Shea Stadium in less than eighteen minutes. From the stadium, they will walk the half mile or so to Corona Park. Once there, they will run the gauntlet of signs ranging from interpreters' placards offering a multitude of language translation services to virulently anti-Graham messages ("Graham Leads to Hell 800-How-True"; more chillingly, "God Caused 9/11 800-How-True").

The park's vast fields are rapidly filling. Unlike typical seating arrangements for Graham's previous crusades, which were held in arenas or stadiums and where Graham could be seen by all attendees, albeit from afar, there is no central location here. Instead, there are vast areas throughout the park where one can spread a blanket, picnic-style, and view the proceedings on Diamond Vision. These seating arrangements are not a matter of choice for the Crusade's organizers but rather their ingenious solution to what might have been regarded by less intrepid servants of the Lord as a formidable obstacle to their plans: the unavailability of a suitable stadium or a more contained park space with defined lines of sight.

There is actually a much smaller area close to the platform where seats are arranged in rows, many of them reserved for the media, crusade organizers, officials, the many Graham grandchildren and great grandchildren, and a small number available on a first-come basis. Thus, obviously, the earlier one arrives the better one's chance to literally be in Graham's presence. Proximity does not appear to be an issue, however, as many attendees appear to be caught up in the spirit of this historic moment and are content to be participants from afar.

There is, however, one jarring note, though in the aftermath of September 11 understandable: security is tight, and if one leaves the seating area for a matter of minutes, say to use the porta-john facilities, one must go through security anew. On balance though, the mood of all concerned is positive and helpful.

Arthur Bailey This crusade was different from 1957. This one was more church-led, more pastoral, whereas the Madison Square Garden crusade was more business-led, in terms of the top people who were involved. The 1957 crusade was more of a Manhattan project, while 2005 was more citywide. This time there was always the doubt that Billy could do it; there were concerns about his health. So my primary responsibility was to keep the community of faith believing that Billy would be there.

David Epstein   If Mr. Graham had not been able to come, [his son] Franklin was ready to go, as were other evangelists on the Graham team.

At exactly 7:13 P.M. on this warm evening, the venerable Cliff Barrows, who has been with Graham for sixty years, greets the thousands who have assembled on the lawns of Corona Park, in the shadow of the Unisphere, with a sonorous "Good evening." Following the showing of a video, Dr. A. R. Bernard, pastor of the Christian Cultural Center, Brooklyn, New York, and chairman of the Crusade's executive committee, steps to the rostrum and, in welcoming remarks observing that "tonight we are part of history," conveys the certainty that this Crusade will become the capstone of Graham's sixty years of ministry to spiritually hungry human beings throughout the world, represented here in microcosm. Characterizing Graham as "one of God's generals," Bernard asks rhetorically, "What better place to do it than at the crossroads of the world, New York City?" Scanning the great crowd assembled before him in the heat of this late June evening, he exclaims, "God is alive and well in New York City!"

Graham understands this welcome religious phenomenon and so is confident in the message he will deliver over the next three days; witness his observation just prior to the Crusade's opening, during an interview with MSNBC's Joe Scarborough:

> New York is a city of neighborhoods. Everybody here belongs to his own neighborhood, and so you don't have the differences as united as they normally would be in a smaller city. And I found out years ago that you have to speak to New Yorkers within their own setting of where they live; and their ethnic background, their language background, their cultural background. And the Gospel speaks to all of them. And I know that when the Gospel is proclaimed, that people will respond. And they do, *always.*

The Reverend Lane Adams, former associate evangelist, BGEA
Billy could get up and quote the telephone book and give an invitation, and people would come to know Christ. Why did God do that, I don't know. And neither does Billy.

Saturday

It is 6:00 P.M. on day two of Billy Graham's last crusade. As the huge crowd gathered throughout Corona Park awaits this evening's opening event, the heat seems to increase, its intensity magnified by the throbbing beat of the musical selections, which obviously have been chosen to attract a younger crowd. In fact, this evening has been designated Youth Night. The city's mayor, Michael Bloomberg, a Republican, and Senator Charles Schumer, a Democrat—who will stay for the entire program—are introduced. In his greetings, the mayor says, "It is a tremendous privilege to welcome Billy Graham to New York City." The mayor goes on to note that among the participants in this Crusade are "visitors from New York and from outside the city who have respect for one another's beliefs and cultures . . . in all our diversity, we appreciate others' faiths. Our city was built on diversity."

Then Graham appears. To great applause, he says, "I was asked by someone in the media if this was our last Crusade. I said, 'It probably is *in New York*. But I also said, 'I never say *never*.'"

The Reverend Henry Holley, director of Asian Affairs, BGEA; accompanied Graham on visits to China and North Korea Some people are dead *before* they're dead. If Billy had the physical energy today, he'd love to get back out there in crusade stadiums. Billy Graham doesn't want to die until he's *dead*.

Graham goes on to note: "The United Nations met here, in Flushing Meadow, for the first five years of its existence. It was also here that the UN voted to establish the State of Israel. It was *right here!*"

Although the huge crowd has afforded Graham a standing ovation, there is a sense of anticipation as to whether Bill Clinton and his wife, Hillary (who is also New York's junior senator), will appear.

Earlier in the week, during the question-and-answer portion of his press conference at the Rainbow Room, Graham found himself in an area of controversy that has dogged him since his emergence as an international figure: when asked whether the debt of African nations should be forgiven, he declined to commit himself, saying, "I don't want to get into politics, but I'm in favor of anything we can do to get them out of poverty." Moments later, however, in discussing the coming Crusade, he appeared to be offering a political endorsement of sorts when he announced, "I've invited Bill Clinton. I hope he will come . . . I love them both." Explaining his reason for caution, he said, "If I get up and talk about some political issue, it divides the audience, and I want to unite." Then, acknowledging that he had erred in the past, he confided "I went too far."

The Clintons have accepted Graham's invitation, and now, on this Saturday evening, they suddenly appear, unannounced, on the platform. They receive a standing ovation—greater even than the one afforded Graham—and are seated. The huge crowd's ovation is hardly lost on Billy Graham. He is a great evangelical leader but also a consummate showman: he knows that the tens of thousands of people gathered here want the Clintons *now* and so he interrupts his own remarks to introduce them, saying, "It's been a great privilege for me to know President Clinton and Senator Clinton. It's hard for me to call them president and senator because I've known them as Bill and Hillary for so long, and I admire both of them. President and Mrs. Clinton have been wonderful friends for many years. I've been very close to both of them. They're a great couple."

Then Graham concludes his introduction by saying, "Many years ago, President Clinton had just addressed an audience that I was going to speak to. I told him, before the audience, that when he left the presidency he should become an evangelist because he has all the gifts and he could leave his wife to run the country." The audience, loving this prospect, erupts in an enormous burst of cheers.

Bill Clinton responds: "I want to tell you all what an honor it is for me to be here as a person of faith. He [Billy Graham] is about the only person I have ever known who has never failed to live his faith. When I was a young man and he came to Little Rock, we had just had a terrible crisis over school integration and the schools were closed. Some powerful white people tried to get Billy Graham to speak to a segregated audience, and he said that he wouldn't come unless everyone could sit together."

A highlight of any Billy Graham Crusade is the evangelist's many humor-filled, often self-deprecating anecdotes. Corona Park is no exception. Among his favorites:

Many years ago, I was on an elevator in a Philadelphia hotel when a man boarded and said, "I hear Billy Graham is on here." Dr. John Sutherland Bonnell, pastor of the Fifth Avenue Presbyterian Church in Manhattan, pointed in my direction and said, "Yes, there he is." The man looked me up and down for about ten seconds and said, "My, what an anticlimax."

At the Garden in 1957, I would preach for almost an hour. But here in Corona Park, my sermons will be considerably shorter. I haven't preached or given a talk since last September. I'm reminded of the man who was supposed to preach for twenty minutes but after forty minutes he was still speaking. Then someone threw a gavel at him and hit a lady seated in the front row in the head, knocking her almost unconscious. She said, "Hit me again; I can still hear him."

Here's a story I told at the Garden in 1957, before most of you here were born. A man from Texas went to a race track. Being a Baptist, he couldn't place a bet. As he stood around the area where the horses were being readied to go out on the track, he saw a Catholic priest talking to a horse. When the race began, the horse broke out ahead and easily won. The man from Texas observed the priest three more times talking to horses and each time the horse won. So the man thought: this is not betting; it's a sure thing. When he saw the priest talking to a horse before the next race, he went out and wagered all the money he had in his pocket. The race began and the horse started out beautifully. But midway down the track it fell and dropped dead. The man went over to the priest and said, "I've watched you talk to four horses and each one won their race. But just now the horse you talked to died." The priest looked at the man and said, "You're not a Catholic, are you?" The man said, "How did you know that? I'm a Baptist." "Well," said the priest, "It's obvious that you don't know the difference between a blessing and the last rites."

It seems that a survivor of the great Johnstown, Pennsylvania, flood—a man who liked to incessantly describe his experiences—died and went to heaven. Once there, he was asked what he would like to do. The man replied, "I would like to give a lecture on the Johnstown flood." "That's fine," he was told, "but remember, Noah is in the audience."

Sunday

The Reverend Howard O. Jones, associate evangelist, retired, BGEA
Billy called and asked me to come to the Crusade. When my son and I walked in to greet him, he grabbed my hand and said, "Howard, you were with me from the beginning, you remember." I sat in the audience with other team members. When Billy asked the crowd to "Pray for England; that's where we are going next," some of us looked at each other as if to say, We wonder if this will happen.

As Billy Graham stands before the ninety thousand people who braved the oppressive heat and humidity of this late June afternoon to hear what is likely to be his final public message, he surely must be experiencing a sense of satisfaction—that if this is to be his evangelical last hurrah, it will be occurring on a very high note.

Billy's sermon this afternoon is not only considerably longer than those of Friday and Saturday, but more coherent and powerful, and he appears to be gaining strength as the afternoon wears on. The blazing sun, the soaring temperature, the very vastness of the setting notwithstanding, he rises to this unique occasion like a great athlete nearing the end of his career who scores that crucial extra point at the end of the game—Arnold Palmer hitting an eagle during his last competitive PGA round, or Ted Williams of the Red Sox smacking a home run into Fenway Park's bleachers in his last time at bat.

———————

Maurice Rowlandson   I think he was a bit worried whether he had the strength to see the three days through. The first night he was extremely careful; the second he expanded a bit; and the third day he was letting it all go. He has always said that he would like to die at a crusade. But you have to face the fact that there came a time when his own team realized he hadn't the strength to do it anymore. New York was a good finish.

———————

In the final accounting, more than 260,000 attend the three-day Crusade, of whom approximately eight thousand come forward at Billy's invitation, either to register decisions for Christ or to recommit their lives to His service.

Mere statistics hardly reveal the whole story, however. Throughout his ministry, Graham preached to huge crowds, with well over a million people having changed their lives in response. In the two years just prior to his New York Crusade, he broke single-day attendance records at Riverfront Stadium, in Cincinnati, and at Texas Stadium, in Irving; preached to an almost-capacity crowd at the Rose Bowl; and produced an enormous response in Kansas City. Thus huge crowds and bumper crops of inquirers were hardly unheard of, even in the final years of Billy's Crusade ministry.

The Corona Park event of June 2005 would prove to be different, however. From the media's reverence at the pre-Crusade press conference to the choir's last rendition of *Just as I Am,* the erstwhile North Carolina farm boy touched New York City to its core.

———————

Gerald Beavan, professor and registrar, Northwestern Schools, Minneapolis, Minnesota; close associate of Graham's   It had to end sometime. You can write scenarios for a dozen different endings and many of them would have been anywhere near as good or nice and wonderful as this. It was a great way to end.

Bill Brown, former president, World Wide Pictures; member, BGEA
He wouldn't continue if he felt his effectiveness was not there. I think he realized his age—that people would come out of respect to hear him and to see him. But they would not see the same Billy Graham you saw in Yankee Stadium [in 1957]. I think he realized that something less

effective might mar that. In some ways, he is probably wise living off the respect and the reputation that people have for him rather than doing something that is beyond his strength and his health.

Michael Deaver, longtime associate of Ronald W. Reagan's; deputy chief of staff during the Reagan presidency   I don't believe Billy has had his last crusade; I believe there is energy in him. I haven't seen him for a year, but as long as he can speak he will be doing it in some way or another. Maybe not standing up at some large stadium; maybe technology will bring him to us in different ways.

Henry Holley   There is great value in the potential of the Internet, but I don't know if it will ever take the place of the simple proclamation to an audience. I hope not; there are certain dynamics that the Holy Spirit can work with in a large stadium where someone stands and proclaims the Gospel. You can use all the technology that God has revealed and use the Internet to have people come to a crusade.

When he left Corona Park, I'm sure he knew it was the end— although there was an invitation to come to England. Billy prayerfully considered that; but upon reflection he decided that he should not accept, so it must have been a very painful experience to know that Corona Park was the last. It would be a thrill if he could come to one of Franklin's festivals. It would also be good for Billy; he is energized when he is with people. I know that Franklin wants him to come any- where he feels like he can come. I think it would be the best thing in the world for Billy; let's pray that will happen.

Chapter Two

FROM CHARLOTTE TO WHEATON

The man who would one day preach to more people in history than any other pastor, evangelist, priest, or pope was born in a white frame house on the three-hundred-acre Graham Brothers Dairy Farm in Charlotte, Mecklenburg County, North Carolina, on November 7, 1918, just four days before the armistice marking the end of the First World War would go into effect. Named Billy Frank, he was the first-born son of Morrow and Franklin Graham, who were pious Presbyterians. Years later, their daughter, Jean, would describe her parents as "people of prayer and utter integrity who lived godly, Biblically based lives in the community."

Billy Frank's parents also had a military heritage: Morrow's maternal grandfather and her husband's paternal grandfather had fought in the Civil War. Now, in the fourth day of his life, as Billy Frank lay in his crib, thousands of flag-waving residents of Charlotte were celebrating the war's end with a parade. The next evening, the visiting Paris Symphony Orchestra would perform in concert at the city's auditorium. Amid the cheering and relief at war's end, however, was the somber realization that 106 soldiers from the county had died in combat and others succumbed to Spanish influenza before they could come home.

Although Billy Frank would later recall that in his childhood his father "eked out a bare existence," Frank Graham was relatively prosperous, so much so that the family was able to survive when, during the height of the Great Depression, the Farmers and Merchants Bank failed and they lost their savings.

Frank, a shrewd trader of cattle and automobiles, managed the farm, while Morrow did the bookkeeping; Frank's brother, Clyde, with whom he had inherited the place, operated the milk processing house.

As a youngster, Billy Frank, along with his brother, Melvin, and two sisters, Catherine and Jean, performed chores both before and after school. Billy Frank's main task was the twice-daily milking of twenty cows. He also worked in the fields and, on occasion, helped deliver the milk to retail customers in town. During those years, Billy Frank was influenced by Reese Brown, the farm's African American foreman, a former Army sergeant whom he would describe in later years as "one of the strongest men I ever saw. He had a tremendous capacity for work and great intelligence. He had a profound effect on my life in its earliest years."

The long hours of hard physical labor notwithstanding, Morrow and Frank placed great importance on spiritual matters. The Graham children were required to memorize the 107 questions of the *Shorter Catechism,* a compendium of the Calvinist doctrine to which their parents devoutly subscribed. The children also memorized scripture verses. The very first passage Morrow Graham taught Billy Frank was Proverbs 3:5–6: "Trust in the Lord with all thine heart; and lean not unto thine own understanding. In all thy ways acknowledge him, and he shall direct thy paths." The children also joined their parents in daily prayer and Bible reading. As the children matured, Morrow and Frank's faith intensified and the atmosphere of their home became one of deepening commitment to Biblical principles and their practical applications.

Despite his religious obligations, Billy Frank managed to find time for more worldly pursuits, such as racing around Charlotte in his father's automobile, dating several local belles (never going further than kissing), and playing baseball. Though he aspired to play in the big leagues, his performance could well have been described as "good field, no hit." One can only wonder what course post-World War II Christianity might have taken had Billy Frank been capable of attaining his dream.

During the spring of 1934, thirty members of the Charlotte Christian Men's Club met in the pasture of the Graham Brothers Farm for a day of prayer and fasting. While Morrow, along with the members' wives, prayed in the new brick house Frank had built to accommodate his growing family, Vernon Patterson, the club's leader, prayed that "out of Charlotte the Lord would raise up someone to preach the Gospel to the ends of the earth." That meeting led to inviting Mordecai Fowler Ham, an old-time fire-and-brimstone preacher with a disposition toward racism and anti-Semitism, to conduct an eleven-week revival beginning in late August.

To be sure, the Charlotte group's invitation had nothing to do with Ham's racism and Jew baiting. Rather, they believed that the flamboyant preacher could follow up the revival that Billy Sunday had held in Charlotte a decade earlier.

One might wonder whether there was need for a revival. Charlotte had one of the highest concentrations of churches per capita in the nation; in fact, the very church the Grahams attended was the largest "country" congregation in the United States. The Depression had taken a spiritual as well as financial toll, however, and Frank Graham and his friends believed that their community was in need of a healthy dose of the old-time religion.

Billy Frank, then sixteen years old, viewed the men who gathered for prayer at his father's farm as "fanatics" and at first expressed little interest in attending Ham's meetings. But when the son of one of Frank's farm workers asked him to drive a truckload of people to the revival, he agreed; remaining for the evening's meeting, Billy Frank came away fascinated. As he recalled in his autobiography *Just as I Am*: "I have no recollection of what he preached about, but I was spellbound. In some indefinable way, he was getting through to me. I was hearing another voice, as was often said of Dwight L. Moody when he preached: the voice of the Holy Spirit. . . . The next night all my father's horses and mules could not have kept me from getting to that meeting."

Attending night after night, Billy Frank became convinced that of the five thousand people seated in the wood-and-steel-framed tabernacle, Ham's message and finger were pointed directly at *him*. In fact, Billy Frank's discomfort was so great that he and his high school friend Grady Wilson decided to join the choir because they would be then sitting *behind* Ham rather than *facing* him. One evening, as the conviction of sin and the need for personal redemption overcame him, Billy Frank walked forward and stood with the more than three hundred people who gathered at the platform. There, a kindly family friend helped him make his decision for Christ.

The following year, Billy Frank, who before his conversion considered attending the University of North Carolina, began classes at the staunchly fundamentalist Bob Jones College (later a university, founded by Bob Jones Sr., a no-nonsense practitioner of the old-time verities), located on the eastern slope of the Appalachians in Cleveland, Tennessee. Billy Frank was joined there by Grady and his brother T. W. Wilson. At Bob Jones College, it was "the founder's way or the highway."

Rev. Charles Massey, classmate of Graham's at Florida Bible Institute; U.S. Army chaplain, retired Billy was an effective preacher. He emulated Bob Jones Sr. with his hand maneuvers, and he had a rapid-paced delivery that was specific to him because of the time he had spent at Bob Jones College.

Rev. Billy Kim, president, Far East Broadcasting Company; former president, Baptist World Alliance; interpreter for Graham at 1973

Seoul Crusade   When I was a student at Bob Jones University, we were told every day in chapel that Billy Graham was a new evangelical and that we should not pray for him. Dr. Bob [Bob Jones Jr.] was so engrossed in fundamentalism that he didn't believe you were supposed to fellowship with anyone who did not believe as you did. There also must be some jealousy in his reaction to Billy Graham. I cannot judge a person's motives, but he always told us that Billy Graham is inclusive, not exclusive—that Mr. Graham invited everyone to be on his platform.

The press asked Mr. Graham that question when he came to Korea. He answered that he could not examine everyone before he began a crusade. His view was that if a person believed what he preached, then let him come hear the Gospel. We were told that if we were part of his ministry, we would be against the will of God. That type of discussion certainly made me think twice before I got deeply involved in the Seoul Crusade. I sought the advice of several of my close friends in the United States who had had a great influence on me and they said that I should interpret for Mr. Graham so that the Korean people would clearly understand his message. My wife, Trudi, who is an American, also encouraged me to participate in the crusade.

As Billy Frank chafed under the college's rigorous spiritual and personal discipline and became prone to bouts of influenza, he began to consider other educational options. His mother had read of, and been impressed by, the curriculum of the Florida Bible Institute, a small, academically unaccredited, Biblically oriented school in Temple Terrace, just outside of Tampa. In late January 1937, Billy Frank arrived on campus.

Charles Massey   Billy cut a swath on the campus right away. He had a personality such that if he walked into a room, you would turn around to see who he was. He was a very charismatic individual, a handsome fellow, always well-dressed, and he made friends quickly.

Billy defrayed some of his expenses by caddying and washing dishes. There he would grow spiritually and dedicate his life to full-time Christian service.

Charles Massey All of us had to work. Tuition was thirty dollars a month and we could work fifteen of that off. Billy did a lot of yard work, washed dishes, and worked in the kitchen. It was a busy time.

Billy, as he now styled himself, benefited from the mentoring of two extraordinary people, Dr. W. T. Watson, the Florida Bible Institute's founder and president; and the Reverend John Minder, the dean of men, who also served as pastor of the Tampa Gospel Tabernacle. In addition, Billy became acquainted with several well-known preachers and evangelists who either vacationed or lectured at the institute.

Charles Massey The students used to have a joke—that the Lord called all these big names south to Florida in the middle of the winter. There was one right after another, and they had an impact upon all of us because most of us were not accustomed to that quality of Bible teacher. It was outstanding for us that these people would come and spend time with us. The institute was like a large family and student activities were like family activities.

Billy was soon honing his preaching style in small churches, street meetings, and trailer parks; he gained confidence in his ability to communicate the Gospel and was buoyed by the impressive number of people who came forward at his invitation to receive Christ.

His one unhappy experience in Florida involved a personal relationship. He had fallen in love with Emily Cavanaugh, a comely and much-sought-after fellow student. Emily seemed to reciprocate his feelings, but on Class Night in May 1938 she gently yet firmly told Billy that she was in love with Charles Massey, who was also a deeply spiritual young man.

Charles Massey My wife [Emily] was engaged to him. We would think now that it was a bit narrow-minded, the way they [the school's administration] treated us. Relationships, while not frowned upon, were well-regulated and you could only date a girl for fifteen minutes, in the lounge, *before* dinner.

During his years in Florida, Billy also changed his religious denomination. Under the guidance of Dr. Minder and Cecil Underwood, the latter a pastor within the

Southern Baptist Convention, he was baptized by immersion. A few months later, in February 1939, Billy was ordained a Southern Baptist minister at Underwood's Peniel Baptist Church, near Palatka, Florida. Now, set apart for the preaching of the Gospel, Billy sought new opportunities to serve God.

Although he received a thorough grounding in Scripture at the Florida Bible Institute, Billy realized the need to continue his education at a faith-based, academically accredited college. He listened intently when, at the institute's graduation ceremony in June 1940, the valedictorian commented that God had chosen ordinary men—like Martin Luther, John Wesley, and D. L. Moody—as human instruments "to shine forth His light in darkness." "The time is ripe; there is room for another name on this list," the speaker concluded.

———————

Charles Massey   Florida Bible Institute gave us an appreciation for learning besides the Bible. At the institute, the Bible was the focus in everything; even the *non*-Biblical courses were Bible-centered. A number of us, like Billy, went on to colleges for liberal arts. And some of us went on to graduate school; I studied at Harvard and Indiana University as well. We felt that the Bible college experience was really not sufficient.

———————

Billy would always regard with great fondness his years at the Florida Bible Institute, now called Trinity College. As he was later quoted in Bill W. Lanpher's *He Is Able,* "I had spent three glorious, happy, character-building, life-changing years in the spiritual atmosphere of the institution. Trinity gave me my beginning in evangelism. My first sermon was preached while a student there. I was encouraged at all times to preach wherever possible. I pitied the poor audiences that had to listen, but the Lord blessed even in those days with souls. I remember praying one night at Trinity, 'Lord, I do not want to be a great preacher, but I do want to be a great soul winner.'"

Billy's goal of attending an accredited four-year college was facilitated by two men from the Midwest: Elner Edman, the brother of V. Raymond Edman, the interim president of Wheaton College, located twenty miles from Chicago's Loop, which was then the nation's premier evangelical academic institution; and Paul Fischer, a Chicago-based lawyer whose brother served as chairman of Wheaton's board of trustees. During the previous winter, while spending several vacation days at the institute, they had heard Billy preach at the Tampa Gospel Tabernacle.

———————

Charles Massey   Most of us went to speak at various churches in Tampa and St. Petersburg. Life has changed; you don't find street meetings anymore. But we went out on the street corners. We would have a quartet, or other type of singing group, and attract quite a crowd. Most of the time, we gave very short, testimony-type messages.

———————

With Fischer taking the lead, he and Edman both pledged to help Billy defray his first-year expenses. Buoyed by Edman and Fischer's generosity and by the blessing of his parents (who knew one of Wheaton's professors), Billy arrived on the Wheaton campus in September 1940 and enrolled as a second-semester freshman.

———————

Helen Stam Fesmire When he came to Wheaton, he was a very quiet person. I would see him on campus and then got to know him when he roomed with my future husband, Lloyd Fesmire. He was just like a farm boy; he didn't stand out right away. At Wheaton he was normal, just like any other student. He didn't push himself or act like he was somebody who was someday going to be a wonderful evangelist. He was a very normal, humble person, and it took time for people to get to know him. He didn't think he was somebody great. I don't think he has ever felt that way about himself. He is a humble servant of the Lord, and this is probably one of the reasons he has been used so well.

The Reverend Dr. Dale Kietzman, schoolmate of Graham's at Wheaton College; professor, William Carey International University, Pasadena, California; in 1990 recommended to the North Korean ambassador to the United Nations that Graham be invited to North Korea Dr. Edman's home was on the campus, and he knew a lot of students by their first names. I learned to drink coffee without sugar because of him; we were seated together at a banquet and he said, "Sugar makes coffee taste like medicine." He taught only one course, but you heard him frequently at the required daily chapel.

Billy was an upperclassman when I entered Wheaton College in 1942. People recognized him on campus. He was slightly older than the average student. He already had an entourage. I was aware of Grady Wilson being there and boosting him. Grady was trying to get Billy elected president of one of the campus literary societies.

Roger Palms, assistant editor, associate editor, and editor, *Decision* magazine, official publication of the BGEA I remember saying to

Billy once, "I meet so many people who were your classmates at Wheaton College; that must have been a large class." He laughed and said, "Actually it was a pretty *small* class."

———————

Given credit for some of his Florida Bible Institute Bible courses, Billy decided to major in anthropology. This decision was a crucial factor in enabling him—a farm boy brought up in what was then the segregated south—to learn of, and understand, other cultures and peoples, given that Wheaton's student body was much larger and more diverse than that of the Bible Institute and represented a cross section of America. Young, spiritually aware, and intellectually challenged by a faculty composed mainly of professional educators, many of Wheaton's students prepared there for careers in full-time Christian service; others came to play active lay roles in their churches and communities.

———————

Anna-Lisa Madeira, née Beckman, classmate of Ruth Bell Graham and Billy Graham's, Wheaton College; founder and member, Carolers for Christ, quartet on "Songs in the Night" radio program I met him as soon as I went to Wheaton. We didn't know he was going to be famous, but we certainly knew he was a wonderful, wonderful person. I was organist and pianist at the Tab [Wheaton Gospel Tabernacle]. We met in a Masonic hall that was always jammed on Sundays, primarily with students, although there were others as well. He came across as a very genuine Christian and you couldn't help but be impressed; he was an excellent preacher. He wasn't *unanimated* when he preached at the Tab and at Western Springs, but he wasn't jumping all over the place either. It wasn't a gymnastic feat, but there was life when he preached in the pulpit, not what we think of some evangelistic preaching—not a Billy Sunday, for instance.

Dale Kietzman   There were churches other than the Tab that students could go to—particularly the College Church and the Bible Church. I went to the Bible Church in the morning and the Tab in the evening. The evening service at the Tab was the place to be; that was where you heard Billy Graham preach. His preaching was very energetic. I assumed he would become a pastor. In fact, I attempted to get him to be a candidate at a church in Indiana when he was a student, but they felt they didn't want him because he had no experience.

Joyce Mostrom, née Ferrin, daughter of Dr. Howard Ferrin, former president, Providence [Rhode Island] Bible Institute; classmate, with her future husband, Don Mostrom, of Ruth Bell and Billy Graham's, Wheaton College; member, Carolers for Christ, quartet on "Songs in the Night" radio program   Wheaton was a truly Christian campus. One was aware that there were some people who didn't believe as others, but I really felt that most everybody truly wanted to please the Lord and to walk with him. There were a lot of us who were dedicated. We were part of a group of people who, especially during the war, went into Chicago. We would sit in train stations to strike up conversations with people about the Lord or ride the El trains and do the same. That was during the war, and people were serious; they were looking for something. On the campus, this group of people who were interested in witnessing would meet on Friday evenings and share how things had gone and have prayer together. The group grew to include seventy to eighty people. People were serious about things of the Lord. I think people were looking to know what their calling in life was. Of course, in those days, one expected a calling to last a lifetime. Nowadays it lasts maybe five or six years and then it changes.

Dale Kietzman   Women were in the majority of the twelve hundred students. The men lived off campus, so campus life was somewhat different than right after the war, when men's dorms were built. Midway through my freshman year, a whole group of men who were in the Navy V-12 program were sent off to Michigan for training. At the end of a semester, whole groups would suddenly be gone.

————————

Wheaton was also at the center of a developing theological ferment that would gain ascendancy within evangelicalism in the post–World War II world. The older fundamentalism, still championed by Bob Jones, John R. Rice, and other diehards, was coming under increasing attack by a group of college and seminary professors who walked a fine line between the liberalism of the mainline denominations and the obscurantism of their leadership. In the coming years, Billy would play a decisive role in the emergence of what came to be known as "the new evangelicalism."

As Billy began his course work, however, he and his fellow students were more concerned with both attaining good grades and finding their life partner. In the months prior to the onset of the war, Wheaton was a safe haven, where Billy flourished, growing spiritually and gaining a better understanding of the workings of God's world. As he had done in Florida, Billy earned spending money through a series of part-time jobs, including helping a classmate, Johnny Streator, operate a one-vehicle trucking business, the Wheaton College Student Trucking Service. Billy also had a number of preaching opportunities throughout the Midwest, assignments requiring many hours of sermon preparation, not to mention considerable travel. As a result, his grades fell. They declined further in the summer of 1941, when he replaced Edman, his mentor who had become Wheaton's incumbent president, as pastor of Wheaton's United Gospel Tabernacle. The congregation consisted mostly of students and faculty. Billy, who preached on Sunday mornings and evenings, as well as at Wednesday evening prayer meetings, was now required to devote even more time to sermon study, as well as to counseling and visitation.

Joyce Mostrom   At the Tab every Sunday night, there was a group of young people who went to the county jail and led a service. I don't remember Billy doing that, but I know that it was under his leadership. Both Don and I were part of the group that went to the county jail. And then we would go up to the campus afterwards and have a candlelight dinner. Don says, "We got to know one another in DuPage County Jail, where Billy Graham sent us."

Helen Stam Fesmire   Our conversations with Billy were about spiritual and campus matters. When he took over the Tabernacle, he was the one to do it, the natural person to take Dr. Edman's place. I heard him say how difficult it was to think that he was preaching to some of his professors. That was always a challenge to him. Billy asked my fiancé, Lloyd, to come with him and lead the singing.

At that time, Billy was distracted from his duties, albeit for a most welcome reason: his attention was riveted on Ruth Bell, a fellow student to whom he had been introduced by Johnny Streator. Interested in missionary work in China, Johnny knew of Ruth's background as the daughter of Dr. L. Nelson Bell and his wife, Virginia, missionaries who had served in China from 1916 until the outbreak of the Second World War, in North Kiangsu province, where he was the director of the Tsingkiang General Hospital. Ruth attended school in Pyongyang, North Korea, and on the Bells's return to the United States she completed high school in Montreat, North Carolina, a small mountain town outside Asheville, where the family spent a furlough year in the mid-1930s.

Helen Stam Fesmire   Billy told Lloyd that there was this girl he liked named Ruth who lived in Scott House, and he asked Lloyd to set up a date with her. But there were *two* students named Ruth living there and Lloyd didn't know which Ruth Billy meant. After the date, Billy said to Lloyd, "That was the *wrong* Ruth! I didn't have a date with the right Ruth." But after that he got the *right* Ruth.

Anna-Lisa Madeira   Ruth was my age; I had already spent a year at a business school and three years at a Bible school. She was also older than the general run of kids who go to college right after high school. There was a maturity there that was different from most of the students.

Helen Stam Fesmire   When we lived at Scott House, Ruth had a roommate. We then moved to Dr. Welsh's house, where four of us, including Ruth, shared the upstairs. Ruth had a room by herself because she could study and think better. She is a private person, a very intelligent, loving, kind person, a very good friend. I think the fact that she had been in China for most of her life before coming to Wheaton showed. She was feisty then but perhaps has become more so.

After Lloyd and I started going steady and Billy and Ruth did too, we saw more of each other. We would usually eat together. Once, a lady professor said to Lloyd, "You know, it doesn't seem right that you four are always eating together. You should be eating with other people so you can share your lives with them instead of just the four of you." We knew what she meant, but it was still nice to eat together.

Anna-Lisa Madeira   Our quartet would often travel to meetings with Billy. He was always pleasant to be with and we all enjoyed being together. It was a blessing to be with him and [George] Beverly Shea. It was a lovely experience, which I treasure. There wasn't any pomp and circumstance; he was just a very nice person. I remember the first Sunday I was there [at Wheaton]; I was a total stranger in town, and Billy and Ruth took me to the home of the Lanes, who would host students after church.

Joyce Mostrom   I thought that Ruth was one of the most beautiful, dearest ladies that I had met. We knew them mainly through the church. They were very much admired. I knew Billy as a preacher and on occasion I was able to contribute a special singing number in the church service.

Anna-Lisa Madeira   You couldn't help but notice [Ruth] when she crossed the campus because she stood out as so different from the other women. Most of us had our permanents and sort of longish hair. Of course, she had long hair, but she wore it straight back with a nice bun at the nape of her neck. Most of us couldn't have worn our hair that simply. She really was an absolutely beautiful woman.

Ruth, who in the estimation of her Wheaton housemother had "the most beautiful Christian character of any young person I have ever known," fell in love with Billy at first sight. Despite their strong mutual attraction, however, Ruth and Billy actually had little in common in terms of life experiences and ambition beside their Christian faith. Ruth was planning to spend her life as a missionary in Tibet, whereas Billy was looking forward to pursuing evangelistic work in America. Yet despite her strong determination to serve abroad, as well as her initial hesitation in making a commitment, Ruth eventually agreed to marry Billy and follow his lead in their life's work. Her decision was likely prompted by a chance encounter at a prayer meeting a mere few days after she and Billy had met. "I had never heard anyone pray like [that] before; I sensed that here was a man that knew God in a very unusual way."

Anna-Lisa Madeira   When they were discussing Ruth's plans to become a missionary in Tibet, Billy kind of put her in her place: he insisted that if they were going to be married, she would have to follow wherever God called him. I guess she became convinced of it—and his mission field became far greater than Tibet. Serving in Tibet would have been wonderful if that is where God wanted him. But obviously, he knew that God didn't want him there and Ruth had to decide. When she met Billy, she just knew he was the man, so if she knew this then she did have to follow where he felt God was calling him.

Millie Dienert   She [Ruth] *wanted* to be a missionary, but, as she would sometimes say, "I'm not sure that's where God wanted me, so God gave me a mission field of my own." That is the way Ruth looked at everything, and that is why she was such a blessing to her husband. God gave him a terrific woman. Certainly, she was appointed by the Lord to be his wife. There is no question about it.

———————

Ruth and Billy married in Montreat on August 13, 1943. Fifty years later, Billy would recall that day as "the most memorable" of his life.

———————

Anna-Lisa Madeira   I was invited to their wedding, but I couldn't afford to go. They did send me an actual wedding photograph.

———————

In September 1945, little more than two years following their marriage, Ruth and Billy became parents with the birth of Virginia, known as "Gigi." Then, at two-year intervals Ruth gave birth to Ann, in 1948; Ruth Bell, in 1950; Franklin, in 1952; and after a six-year hiatus Ned, in 1958.

Ruth's parents, the Bells, would provide their grandchildren with both love and supervision, allowing Ruth to travel with Billy during the early years of his crusade ministry.

———————

Charles Riggs, former crusade director, BGEA, associated with Graham since the late 1940s   Ruth is a Godly woman. She knew what she wanted and demanded that things be done properly. She made sure, *before* a crusade ever began, that everybody was in step.

———————

In time, Ruth decided to remain at Montreat most of the time, in order to supervise the children and provide them with a sense of stability during Billy's frequent absences. She did, however, exert enormous influence from afar on her increasingly well-known and sought-after husband.

———————

Charles Riggs   Ruth had to devote herself to bringing up the children. She was mostly in charge of the children's religious education. Billy's ministry was preaching; training the children was *Ruth's* responsibility.

Helen Stam Fesmire   He was able to leave home and know that he had a wife who would take good care of his children. She would pray for him and carry on at home and be waiting for him to come home again. She played a big part; he couldn't have done it if she weren't the woman that she is. She is a strong woman. That came out more as she had more children and was in charge of the home when he wasn't there.

Anna-Lisa Madeira   Ruth deserves a lot of credit for how she so often went through this all alone in raising the children. But I understand that Billy was home more often than people might think; he did his best at being there as often as he could.

Millie Dienert   Ruth played the most important role that any woman could play. I have never heard that woman complain about her husband's being away in crusade activity, sometimes for one month or for six or seven months at a time. As she was home alone raising her children, she felt that she was as much a part of his ministry in taking care of their family and in being a helpmate to him as if she were with him in the crusades. Ruth shied away from any big fuss about her. She was—and is to this day—a very delightful and wonderful person to know because she was so dedicated to the ministry of her husband; everything she did on behalf of him at home she felt was a ministry.

In addition to helping out with the children during the early years of Graham's ministry, Ruth's father, whom Billy always addressed as "Dr. Bell," was also a trusted adviser and warm friend to Graham and would have a profound influence on the evangelist's life. A lifelong Presbyterian, Bell would expand his son-in-law's appreciation for the status of Christian faith within the mainline denominations, thereby saving him from the narrowness to which many of his contemporaries at Wheaton fell prey.

Gerald Beavan   It's a fair assumption that Dr. Bell was his greatest mentor. He was, like his daughter, a very common-sense person. He would speak very plainly to Billy. Another mentor was Dr. V. Raymond Edman, the president of Wheaton when Billy was a student there. He was a great help to Billy.

In early 1943, as he began to consider what he would do upon graduation that summer, Billy was approached by a Chicago publishing executive, Robert Van

Kampen, who served as a deacon of the Western Springs Baptist Church, located about twenty miles from the Wheaton campus. Van Kampen had heard Billy preach and, sensing his evangelistic potential, asked if he would consider becoming pastor at Western Springs. Accepting Van Kampen's offer, Billy assumed his position during the summer of 1943 and remained there for one year.

The church, renamed at his urging the Village Church out of consideration for the many non-Baptists who resided in the area, was structurally unfinished so the congregation worshipped in a roofed basement. Graham's sermons brought a significant harvest of souls, but he was not quite at home with the more mundane duties of pastoring a church.

_____

Helen Stam Fesmire We were with Billy and Ruth when Billy preached his trial sermon at Western Springs. The people at Western Springs kept after him to come and be their pastor. He finally did say yes, but he didn't talk to Ruth about it. Later he said, "I'll never again make a decision like this without conferring with Ruth."

My husband succeeded Billy at Western Springs. When he was interviewed for the job, he was told that they didn't want a pastor who took other engagements all over the place, as Billy had been doing. He would be at Western Springs for a couple of Sundays and then he'd be off preaching someplace else. Billy was not meant to be a pastor; he was meant to be an evangelist.

_____

While still affiliated with Western Springs, Graham was asked to take over a forty-five-minute Sunday night radio program, "Songs in the Night," produced by Torrey Johnson, a young Chicago pastor; the show was broadcast over the fifty-thousand-watt station WCFL.

_____

Joyce Mostrom Torrey was charismatic and a good communicator. I thought of him as part of a terrific team that worked together.

Anna-Lisa Madeira I don't know whether Billy himself would have thought of having a radio program if Torrey Johnson had not been too busy to continue the program. Of course, God was behind that. The success he had on the radio may have helped him realize that there was more for him to do. He would have sensed that because of the way people responded.

It wasn't like today, where some people may come forward just to get a look at him. This was all genuine; there was then no notoriety about the man to make you want to come forward. He must have realized, with the great humility that has always characterized his life, that God was preparing him and moving him out into bigger and bigger spheres.

Johnson told Graham that he was involved with another radio show and suggested to him that the Village Church should underwrite the "Songs in the Night" weekly budget of $150. Starting in early December 1943, with initial funding from Robert Van Kampen, the program, broadcast live from the Village Church, was an immediate success. Credit for its success was due in no small measure to the rousing renditions of Bev Shea, a bass baritone whom Billy recruited after having barged into the staff singer and announcer's office at WMBI, the radio station of the Moody Bible Institute. Bev Shea would remain as a major—and beloved—personality of the crusade ministry for the remainder of Graham's six-decade-long career.

Paul Ferrin, son of Dr. Howard Ferrin, involved in Graham's Boston and New England Crusades, 1950 and 1951, respectively   My older sister attended Wheaton College and sang on Graham's "Songs in the Night" radio program.

Joyce Mostrom   I was in a women's quartet. We went down every Sunday night on the train to Western Springs. We sang the signature song and perhaps one other selection and the program went back and forth between music and message. Our participation didn't last long because Billy wasn't there long.

Anna-Lisa Madeira   I was the one who started the Carolers for Christ quartet. I had been in a women's quartet at Providence Bible Institute and when I went out to Wheaton I was in the glee club. I asked some of the gals if they would like to be in a quartet. Billy had heard our quartet and, of course, we knew each other very well because I was the organist and pianist in the Tabernacle, so one day he asked me if the quartet would be willing to sing on the program. We thought that would be very nice. It was a lovely program. He didn't preach; he read poetry, he read the Scripture and in and out came the music. Our quartet sang the theme song ["Songs in the Night"] at the beginning and at the end and also sang something in the program itself. We went out every Sunday afternoon by train and would be with him at the Young People's meeting and at the evening service and stay on for the radio program.

In the summer of 1944, he asked if the girls could stay on. I told him I had to go home to earn money for tuition. He asked me to become his secretary for the summer, and I think I am officially the first secretary he ever had. He got me a place to live and different families would feed me at night. I earned twenty-five dollars a week. He was just a very kind, thoughtful person.

In turning "Songs in the Night" over to the young pastor, Johnson not only gave Graham's ministry the opportunity to have an impact beyond the immediate Chicago area but accelerated the up-and-coming evangelist's journey toward achieving his national reputation.

Ben Armstrong   Our first meeting was over lunch in a restaurant on Euclid Avenue, in Cleveland. He was handsome, well dressed, and very articulate. He had a vision for reaching people that very few people I've met have, not only locally but overseas. At that time he had the Chicago-based radio program. What was interesting was that he had the idea that he would be much called of the Lord to do a program that would be national and international. As he shared this vision with me, I felt that this was a person who had more than just an average interest in what later became known as Christian broadcasting.

Helen Stam Fesmire   I don't think we had an idea of what Billy would become in the future; we just didn't think that far ahead. We knew that he was a very good preacher and an evangelist and that there had been a response to his messages. There were people in Western Springs who got saved while he was there.

Anna-Lisa Madeira   We didn't know he was going to be *famous,* but you knew that God was using him and that God was going to continue to use him—and Ruth as well. There was something unique about them; there is no getting around it. And it wasn't flashiness. I guess it was their maturity in Christ and their total commitment to Christ, which was very evident.

Paul Ferrin   Billy Graham came to Providence Bible Institute in 1944. Then he came to our home in Cranston for dinner. I remember him as being tall, lanky, and gawky. He was quite clumsy, I thought. I had been playing high school baseball in those days and he didn't move with the grace I would have liked to have seen in him. He was nice looking, pleasant, and quite stern, even though he had a nice smile. By stern I mean that he gave you the impression that he had something that the world needed and there were no two ways about it. He was not lighthearted about it; he was serious. Perhaps intense, rather than stern, is a better way to describe this.

Joyce Mostrom   That was Billy's introduction to New England. I saw him preach in Providence. He just strode across the stage in a very gangly manner. I knew him well but I thought to myself at the time: there is a lot for him to learn. His style there was different from when he preached at the Tab, a small church where he didn't have room to move on the platform. What struck me was that in Providence his whole demeanor was different. It was different as an evangelist than as a pastor. He was more polished when I saw him preach at Madison Square Garden.

Paul Ferrin   As far as the conversation was concerned, at dinner in my father's house there were only two subjects: theology or sports. My father felt that Graham was quite promising. Graham's reaching out to people meant a lot to Dad. He later arranged for him to come to New England, believing that Graham had a message for the region, notwithstanding the saying that New England was the graveyard of evangelism.

Chapter Three

THE MAKING OF AN EVANGELIST

American society was in ferment during the war years. Especially affected were young people, many of whom either volunteered for military service or were drafted, while their younger siblings were emotionally set adrift as fathers served overseas and mothers worked long hours in defense plants or other war-related jobs.

Torrey Johnson realized the opportunities for evangelism prompted by war and dislocation. He was not alone in his thinking; pastors and church leaders in many American cities understood that a potential harvest of young people existed if only a way could be found to relate the Gospel to them. As thousands of soldiers passed every day through Chicago, which was then the nation's railway hub, the Loop with its many amusement centers attracted young people from the suburbs eager to spend an evening away from the routines and strains of their lives; Johnson believed that his city was potentially fertile ground for spiritual revival.

As the war progressed, Johnson, then pastor of the Midwest Bible Church, on Cicero Avenue, sought venues for youth rallies. His efforts were encouraged by Bev Shea and Lacey Hall, the latter a Moody Bible Institute student, both of whom urged Johnson to do something for the youth of Chicago. As a student seeking to earn money for college tuition, Johnson had shown entrepreneurship by operating an ice business in the summer resort town of Williams Bay, Wisconsin; now, in early 1944, he contracted to lease the three-thousand-seat Orchestra Hall, home of the Chicago Symphony, for twenty-one weeks. There, he would hold a series of Saturday evening youth meetings under the auspices of a group he named Chicagoland Youth for Christ.

So it was on the Saturday evening of May 27, 1944, that Billy Graham, who greatly admired Johnson, spoke at the initial rally. Sick to his stomach and suffering from "the worst fit of stage fright in my life," he preached to a full house on Daniel 5:7 ("Thou are weighed in the balances and found wanting"). Then, when he gave the invitation, forty-two young people came forward to make decisions for Christ.

In mid-November, a group of regional Youth for Christ (YFC) directors from around the country gathered in Detroit, where they created Youth for Christ International, choosing as its motto "geared to the times, anchored to the rock." Johnson was elected chairman of the temporary executive committee. The following year he became the organization's first president. Because of his many commitments elsewhere, however, Johnson realized he would not be able to actually run the nascent group. Turning once again to Graham, whom he encountered in Florida in late December, Johnson asked him to become YFC's vice president and thus its first full-time employee.

Graham, still employed in his pastorate at Western Springs, was then recuperating from a two-month siege of the mumps, an illness that was not only enervating and embarrassing but caused him to abandon his goal of joining the military chaplaincy training program he had applied for in late 1941, following the bombing of Pearl Harbor on December 7.

Helen Stam Fesmire   When Lloyd had a student pastorate in Pennsylvania, Billy was in the area for some meetings and he came to stay with us overnight. In the morning, as we were having breakfast, Billy said, "Oh boy! There's something wrong with my neck, it hurts. I think I'd better get into my car and go home." That was the beginning of his mumps.

At that time, Graham was increasingly at odds with his congregation over the frequent out-of-town preaching engagements. So wide was the breach that the deacons threatened to reduce his forty-dollar weekly salary. One of his friends, who knew of the situation, believes that Graham had particular issues with an important and "exceedingly wealthy" layperson. Later, when Graham became famous, that individual was only too happy to claim him as a friend.

Following prayerful consideration—this time Ruth took part in the decision-making process—Billy opted to accept Johnson's offer. In 1945, his first year at his new post, he visited forty-seven states on behalf of YFC. His rallies featured music—rhythmic gospel tunes and spirituals rather than hymns—as well as preaching, allowing him to become acquainted with scores of young pastors and laypeople who would, down the road, greatly assist his ministry.

William Martin, Harry and Hazel Chavanne Professor of Religion and Public Policy and chairman, Department of Sociology, Rice University; author; authorized biographer of Graham   A key element [of the Graham ministry] was his involvement in Youth for Christ in the 1940s. He became the organization's organizer, traveling around the United States and Europe, making important contacts. So when he went back to places he had visited on behalf of Youth for Christ, he had the help of the vibrant young preachers he had already helped.

Anna-Lisa Madeira   When he was at the Tabernacle, I don't think he could have ever imagined what would later happen. I don't think he had any *idea* that the ministry would become so large. When he went out speaking for Youth for Christ, it probably began to sink in that he had a special gift that God was using and using more and more.

The success of YFC had already attracted the attention of the publishing magnate William Randolph Hearst. Struck by the huge turnout achieved by Johnson at a rally held at Soldier Field, in Chicago, he sent his editor there a telegram instructing him to "Puff YFC."

William Martin   Hearst, and [Henry R.] Luce after him, had made their reputations by being able to match a message designed for a mass audience with a medium designed for a mass audience. And in Billy Graham they saw a person who not only had that talent but was the medium himself. Hearst directed his editors to puff Youth for Christ and sent a reporter along when Billy toured Europe on behalf of YFC.

In the early spring of 1946, Johnson organized the YFC tour of Great Britain and the continent. His six-member team included the song leader Stratton Shufelt and a young but well-known pastor from Toronto, Charles Templeton. Accompanying the evangelists was the Hearst reporter, Wesley Hartzell, whose accounts of the tour published in the *Chicago Herald Examiner* were syndicated nationally by the International News Service.

Gerald Beavan   Chuck Templeton was a far better preacher than Billy ever was. He was a master preacher, but he never quite made it; he didn't have the total dependent faith in God that Billy had. Chuck was a terrific guy. One time we were having meetings in Boston and Chuck had come to visit us. As we were riding in a taxi through some of those winding, narrow streets he made a statement that was so typical of him. He said, "You know, these streets were once just lanes for people to lead their cows. That's why they wander so. When the lanes were hardened into concrete and steel they couldn't be changed but when they were still paths they could have been. That's the way it is with a human life once it gets hardened into sin." He would pop out with these profound comments.

Billy had had no theological education, so to speak. I was kind of the resident theologian for the team. I recall riding on a train to Boston when Billy was going to speak at MIT. He said, "Jerry, give me some philosophical things to say, something about existentialism, or something like that." My counsel to him was, "Billy, stick with the Bible; that's home field advantage to you. Those people know more about philosophy and existentialism than you will ever know. You know more about the Bible than they do; claim that home field advantage." His great phrase in those days was, "The Bible says."

After a fiasco at a military base near Gander, Newfoundland, where their plane was forced down by bad weather (the group was taken for a vaudeville ensemble), the YFC team arrived in London and was driven to the posh Dorchester Hotel. There, Graham and Templeton gazed in wonder at the bidet installed in the bathroom, Billy mistakenly concluding that it was a "foot bath." It was only a matter of time, however, before the group was on the road, their posh surroundings at the Dorchester giving way to the typically unheated halls and homes of England and Scotland.

At that time, Graham and Templeton began a friendship that would be marked by both mutual concern and ever-widening theological differences. So great was their friendship that in a later interview with the author Marshall Frady in *Billy Graham: A Profile of American Righteousness*, Graham would say, "I love Charles to this very day. He's one of the few men I have ever loved in my life. He and I had been so close. But then, all of a sudden, our paths were parting." Years later, as Templeton was suffering through the final stages of Alzheimer's, Graham contacted his son, Brad, and offered a private plane to fly his friend anywhere for medical care. It was too late, however, for him to help Charles Templeton.

In a strange yet likely providential way, Templeton's increasing doubts in the mid-1940s concerning the validity of evangelical faith helped Billy solidify his own faith. Templeton, who had held well-attended rallies at the Rose Bowl in

Pasadena and the Shrine Auditorium in Los Angeles, as well as at Detroit's Olympia and Toronto's Maple Leaf Gardens, went to Montreat in the late summer of 1948 (in Templeton's memoir, 1945 is noted as the year of his visit, but that date is unlikely) and informed Graham, "It isn't possible any longer to believe the Biblical account of creation. The world wasn't created; it has evolved over millions of years."

Billy, who would soon come to struggle with his own beliefs, replied, "I believe in the Genesis account because it is in the Bible. I've discovered something in my ministry: when I take the Bible literally, when I proclaim it as God's word, I have power. When I stand before people and say, 'God says' or 'the Bible says,' the Holy Spirit uses me."

It was during this conversation that Templeton urged his friend to join him as a student at Princeton Theological Seminary. Knowing of that institution's liberal-leaning theological stance, Graham refused. He asked Templeton, "How would it look if a college and seminary president [Graham had assumed those positions at Northwestern Schools in December 1947] went back to school?" Templeton, in his memoir, adds that Graham did offer to accompany him to an overseas university, such as Oxford.

So great were both the need and the response, as evidenced by the spring 1946 tour, that by late September Graham headed back to Britain. During a visit there that would end up lasting six months, the increasingly popular evangelist was joined for part of the time by Ruth, as well as by a young and confident song leader, Cliff Barrows, who joined the group when Stratt Shufelt had to remain at home. Barrows and his wife (who was named Billie) had already conducted successful crusades combining their musical talents and Cliff's considerable preaching skill. Soon after the group's return to the United States, Barrows, Billie, Bev Shea, and Grady Wilson became the nucleus of the Graham team.

Following his return to the States at the beginning of April 1947, Graham came increasingly to the attention of Dr. W. B. Riley, pastor of the First Baptist Church of Minneapolis and president of Northwestern Schools, a Christian institution the pastor had founded there in 1902.

Gerald Beavan   In 1947, I had been invited by Dr. W. B. Riley to come to Northwestern Schools as his assistant—I was a professor of psychology at Northwestern and taught some courses in the seminary—to help him develop a new school of liberal arts. To discuss the possibility, I went out to a Bible conference at a place called Medicine Lake, a few miles out of the city, and one of the speakers at the conference was Billy Graham. I found him to be a nice fellow, a very dynamic preacher. He seemed to be a good guy and I got along quite well with him. Later that year, when

Dr. Riley died, one of his deathbed appointments was that Billy Graham would become president of Northwestern Schools. So suddenly I was working for Billy.

Billy had actually met Riley years before, at the time of a visit by the latter to the Florida Bible Institute campus. Observing Graham's success over the years, Riley became convinced that Graham should succeed him as the president of the Northwestern Schools. In late October, under pressure to accept the post, Graham issued a statement in which he indicated that in the event of an emergency he would consider becoming the institution's *interim* president.

This situation arose when on December 5, 1947, George Wilson, a school official who later served as Billy's key business executive, telephoned the evangelist with the news that Riley had died. Thus it was that the twenty-six-year-old Billy Graham became the nation's youngest college president. Graham and Northwestern Schools never became a good fit, however, and although he maintained an office at the school and attended faculty and board meetings, he entrusted Northwestern Schools' day-to-day operations to Wilson and Gerald Beavan. As Graham explained his ambivalence in a comment to Torrey Johnson, "God's given me one great gift. I have a gift of bringing people to Christ. And that's what I've got to do."

Gerald Beavan   He had absolutely no qualifications to be a college president. He had been to Bob Jones College, did some courses at a Bible school down in Florida, and then went to Wheaton College to finish up and got his bachelor's degree. That was his total educational background, which really doesn't equip you to become president of a Bible school, college, and theological seminary. I think he was hesitant on those grounds, thinking, How can I do this? I got involved with him because he was looking over the qualifications of his faculty and staff and found that I had worked my way through theological seminary by doing radio and advertising publicity work. At that time he was holding little crusades in towns like Altoona, Pennsylvania, so he asked me if I would help him. When he would get to a city, he would send me information about the upcoming series of meetings. I would write a news release and send it out. Then, after the last night of the meetings, he would call me up and tell me what happened and I would write another news release about what had taken place.

Maurice Rowlandson   I was one of ten people from the United King-dom who Billy invited to attend Northwestern Schools. In my two years, Billy came and went. His vice president, T. W. Wilson, and the business manager, George Wilson, were there all the time. Whenever Billy was at the school he made a point of meeting with students. [It should be men-tioned that Gerald Beavan does not recall T. W. Wilson's having spent much time at the school.—authors]

Gerald Beavan   It is not totally fair to say, as some have, that Billy was not a hands-on president. Let's say he was not an *academic* president. He encouraged the growth of the schools, and we did grow considerably. He left the day-to-day administration to the faculty and staff. He did not live in Minneapolis; he would only be there occasionally. He did some innovations. He adopted a slogan for the schools, "knowledge on fire." It was his idea to bring students over from foreign countries to attend the three-year Bible school with the understanding that they would go back and work in their homelands.

In the three years following a winter tour of the British Isles, Graham continued to hold YFC rallies but increasingly conducted his own meetings. Starting in Charlotte in September 1947, he and his team would hold "campaigns." (The term *crusade* came into use only in 1950, when his associate, Willis Haymaker, so characterized a meeting held in Columbia, South Carolina.)

Paul Ferrin   When I attended Billy Graham's meetings in 1950, my heart was just pulsating with joy and happiness. I recall a sermon he preached in Boston. It was on Proverbs 29:1 ("He who is often reproved and hardens his neck will suddenly be destroyed and that without remedy" [NKJV]). His preaching was full of fire and quite bombastic. He was animated beyond belief and looked seven feet tall.

Meanwhile, in 1948 Billy was invited to participate, along with other preachers, in the annual tent meeting conducted by the Los Angeles Christian Business-men's Committee. Johnson, who in those years handled Graham's schedule, wanted him to be the sole speaker. Then in 1949 the Los Angeles group asked Graham to hold a three-week meeting beginning in early September.

Weeks before the scheduled event, in late August, Billy was invited to participate in a conference at Forest Home, a retreat center in the mountains east of
Los Angeles. It was there that he would confront the greatest crisis of his life, as
he and Charles Templeton continued their discussion concerning the inerrancy
of the Scriptures. Mere days before he was to begin the Los Angeles meeting,
Graham—who had had no doubt up to that point concerning the validity of the
Gospel—grappled with the most basic of theological issues: whether or not
the Bible is literally true.

In his autobiography, *Just as I Am,* Billy recounted that crisis, writing, "If I
could not trust the Bible, I could not go on. I would have to quit the school presidency. I would have to leave pulpit evangelism." After pondering many verses of
Scripture containing the phrase "thus saith the Lord," he went for a walk in the
moonlight. He paused at a tree stump, dropped to his knees, and (although he
cannot recall his exact words) prayed, "Oh God! There are many things in this
book I don't understand. There are many problems with it for which I have no
solution. There are many seeming contradictions. There are some areas in it that
do not seem to correlate with modern science. I can't answer some of the philosophical and psychological questions Chuck and others are raising. Father, I am
going to accept this as Thy Word by faith!"

As he rose up, he realized that he had resolved forever his crisis in favor of the
Lord's Word.

———

Lane Adams   On one occasion when I was pastor of the Key Biscayne
Presbyterian Church, Billy and Ruth were staying at the Key Biscayne Hotel.
Billy called and suggested that my wife, Annette, and I join them at the
beach. We did, and while talking to Billy I drew a line in the sand and I said,
"This is my timeline. Here is X, where I was born; here is Y, where I was *born
again.* If I take this line right straight on out to infinity, I will be *here.* All day,
I deal with infinite perfection, and when I measure myself against the Lord
Jesus Christ I'm just covered with guilt because I am so much less than I
ought to be. I seem to mature so slowly. Can you give me any help?"

And with amazing, and characteristic, humility he pulled his line
on the timeline back about three quarters and said, "If you're *there,* I'm
here. The only hope for either one of us is that the blood of Jesus Christ
covers that great gap."

———

September arrived and the Los Angeles meeting began, albeit modestly.

———

Charles Riggs   He was just a beginner in a tent in Los Angeles, and he really did get up and yell a lot, thinking this was the way to get the job done—he was just shouting it out there. But he changed so much after that; he realized it wasn't the shouting that was getting the message across. God knew that he was a man who was going to spread the Gospel everywhere around the world, so God began toning him down to get the message across.

As the pace of the Los Angeles meeting accelerated, it was decided to go beyond the original three-week schedule. Two major factors contributed to the decision to extend the meetings, which would continue for twelve weeks. One had to do with the somewhat sensational conversions of three men of quite diverse backgrounds. The first individual, Stuart Hamblen, was the son of a West Texas preacher and himself the well-known host of a Los Angeles radio program. The second, Jim Vaus, worked as a conductor of wiretaps for the notorious West Coast gangster Mickey Cohen. The third, Louis Zamperini, was a former track star and Olympian whose two-year imprisonment in a Japanese prisoner of war camp had left him depressed and broken in spirit.

Louis Zamperini, former University of Southern California track star; member of the U.S. track team, 1936 Olympic Games; converted at Graham's Los Angeles meeting, 1949   People in the apartment where we lived were talking to my wife and me about a fellow coming out here. Because our marriage was breaking up, she went to hear him. That is how it started.

The second factor—one beyond Graham's immediate control—concerned Hearst's interest in promoting the up-and-coming young evangelist. As he did earlier with reference to Youth for Christ, Hearst sent a telegram to his editors. This time, however, he exhorted them to "Puff Graham."

Louis Zamperini   Billy Graham was unknown, except for church people, and because three well-known people were all saved in the same week—a famous broadcast cowboy, a singer-songwriter; Mickey Cohen's wiretap person; and me, an Olympic athlete—Hearst in New York saw a little article about this and he called the editor of the [Los Angeles]

Examiner here, and says, "Blow up Billy Graham." Otherwise, evangelism was a dirty word in those days. There were so many crooked evangelists leading up to Billy Graham, and here comes an honest, refreshing evangelist, so Hearst realized that something was going on here; he realized that Billy Graham was *real*. When I talked to the editor, he said to me, "Who do you think talked to Hearst?" Meaning: God.

Howard Jones   I believe that it was the sovereignty of God, who for some reason known only to Himself picked Billy to do something in the field of evangelism that no other evangelist was able to do. If you go back to Los Angeles in 1949, the crowds began to dwindle. Billy told me that weariness had crept in. The team met and realized that unless God did something, the meetings would have to end. Little did they realize that a miraculous thing would happen. One morning, they awoke to find Billy's picture on the front page of the newspaper. Billy told us many times that this was the sovereign work of God—that God had touched Mr. Hearst.

Gerald Beavan   Hearst's telegram was very crucial. Up to that point, Billy had been going to small cities; he was active in Youth for Christ and was an itinerant evangelist. In fact, the Los Angeles meeting itself wasn't that big. It wasn't one of the massive meetings he would later conduct. It was held in a tent on the corner of Washington and Hill Streets. But then Hearst, who more or less controlled the Southern California press, sent that famous message to his people and suddenly Billy became a front-page name. That certainly launched him because from that moment on we were able to go to other major cities. ·That is really when his nationwide crusades got started. It was terribly important.

I believe Hearst saw that here was a young man who had an important message, from God if you will, and who could express it well, and meant only good, and Hearst just decided to give Billy a boost.

The astute publisher's order to his minions led first to major coverage in his two Los Angeles newspapers and then to wider circulation throughout the Hearst media empire. By the time the meetings ended on November 20, thousands of people had come forward, either to receive Christ or to recommit their lives. Graham had clearly become a major national personality.

Other Turning Points

"The Hour of Decision"

Billy had radio experience from his having taken over "Songs in the Night" from Johnson. In those hectic days following Los Angeles and his early 1950 tour of New England, however, he did not give much thought to enhancing his ministry through a nationwide radio program. It would take the persistence of two advertising men to accomplish that mission.

Gerald Beavan   Fred Dienert was Walter Bennett's associate. The Walter Bennett advertising agency was headquartered in Chicago. They had a branch in Philadelphia, and Fred Dienert was there. One time, they were at a diner in New Jersey when Fred's father-in-law, Theodore Elsner, who pastored a church in Philadelphia, asked them why they didn't get Billy Graham on the radio. The two of them, in a way of speaking, began to pursue Billy. They said, "We can get you on ABC." They were relentless and finally they came to a crusade which was held in a wooden tabernacle in Portland, Oregon.

That night, Billy said that he had this opportunity to go on radio and, in a Biblical sense, he put out a fleece, naming a certain amount of money that would have to come in. He asked anybody who would like to [do so to] give donations toward getting on the air. Grady would be in a little office area adjoining the tabernacle to receive their gifts, and people were giving him money and checks and he was stuffing them in his pockets and in boxes. Billy had set the number at $25,000. We all went into that little room and counted and it came to $23,500 and everybody said, "This is great." Walter and Fred said, "We'll make up the remaining $1,500." Billy said no. He used a phrase something like this: "The devil could give us $23,500; God will give us $25,000." Walter and Fred checked out of their room and started for the airport, figuring it was over. When they got there they said, "If Billy had this much faith, we ought to go back and stand with him."

Millie Dienert   When God speaks to somebody, it is very difficult to explain except that for no reason at all you did what you did—you just felt it was not time to leave, and to go back. Both of the men were very much in touch with heaven and they had prayed a great deal about the account. They told the Lord that if they were not to have it they didn't want it. I believe it was one of those times when God does speak quietly with a *nudge,* and I believe that nudges come from the Lord. I'm sure that's the way it happened.

Gerald Beavan   When they got back, the only room that they had available in the old Multnomah Hotel was the bridal suite, so these two guys signed up for the bridal suite! We then came back to the hotel from the snack we usually had after the meetings and went over to pick up the mail. There were three envelopes there from people who hadn't been able to get to Grady. They totaled $1,500—bringing it up to the $25,000 Billy had asked for. We went up to Billy's room and signed the contract, and Walter and Fred went back, and that's how "The Hour of Decision" got started.

Millie Dienert   Their persistence was typical of their personalities. They felt that the future of Mr. Graham's ministry was in getting to the people, and not just to a crusade crowd but to a home crowd. They had the vision for that. It was difficult to give that to Mr. Graham because he never decided that he wanted anything big or beyond what God had given him—and that was the crusade ministry. Their persistence came because they were trying to fulfill their responsibility as media people to tell Mr. Graham that he needed to be a voice to all the people and not just crusade people.

God makes no mistakes, and God has the right person at the right time. When God has something in mind, He uses the people *He* wants to use. That was exactly what happened with the men. They just felt that God had given them the urge for Dr. Graham. That's why they kept so persistent about it. They saw a man of simplicity, integrity, honesty, and with an open-hearted desire to see people come to know Jesus Christ. They never saw him deviate; they saw the persistency of his calling as an evangelist being more important to him than anything else. They realized that here was a young man that was satisfied that God was blessing the crusade activity, when there's a big world out there that God has for the man's voice. My husband said over and over again, "I would have backed away and not pressured if I hadn't felt his own heart cry for people to come to know Jesus."

Gerald Beavan   "The Hour of Decision" provided a great resource of prayer and financial support, both of which were absolutely necessary for Billy's ministry to continue. The program linked together millions of people not only in the U.S. but elsewhere in the world. Billy's ministry was not built on a few large gifts; it was built on many small gifts. So "The Hour of Decision" was extremely important in Billy's ongoing ministry. Would there have been one if the other $1,500 hadn't come in? I don't know how you answer that. Obviously, God wanted it to be.

Ben Armstrong   You might say that "The Hour of Decision" had a seminal effect upon his ministry. It was decisive. In that program he initiated a standard of sermonizing that was unique. His first point was to secure the listener to be attentive, so he utilized a famous event of the day. His second point was to spend time talking about his concept of what the Gospel was. The interesting point, which was unique—especially for a young man in 1950—was to ask for the listener's decision to accept Christ as personal savior. That was very unusual. Other programs I had heard at the time would consist of preaching and evangelism but would seldom include a call for a decision. So the "The Hour of Decision" was exactly the right name for what he was trying to do, and that was to evangelize.

He was very persuasive and articulate. He had a southern accent, which made him appear to be somewhat nondirective. His language wasn't confrontational but actually on radio was very confrontational. He was staccato in the way he spoke. His words came quickly. It wasn't the fireside chat that I was used to with President [Franklin D.] Roosevelt; it was much more confrontational. When he presented the evidence, he called for a decision.

The Founding of the Billy Graham Evangelistic Association

Gerald Beavan   The BGEA came into being as a result of the radio contract. Billy didn't have the money to keep the radio program going. You had to receive contributions, which meant that you had to create a 501(c)(3) charitable organization in order to give people tax exemption for making donations. The BGEA got started for that purpose. For our first broadcast, we did a rehearsal in the Municipal Auditorium in Minneapolis during a crusade there, and the actual first time on the air was from Atlanta.

Establishment of the BGEA can also be traced to a meeting involving Graham, Cliff Barrows, George Beverly Shea, and Grady Wilson, held in Modesto, California, in late October 1948. There Graham, who was determined not to repeat mistakes made by previous evangelists, called his close associates together and asked them to separately take an hour to list problems that had sullied evangelism's reputation. When the group reconvened, four major issues ended up on the table. One involved finances; a second sexual impropriety; a third had to do with what Graham referred to as the "tendency of many evangelists to carry on their work apart from the local church, even to criticize local pastors and churches openly and scathingly"; while a fourth revolved around publicity and the practice of some evangelists of exaggerating both the size of their audience and the number of converts.

The "Modesto Manifesto," though never committed to paper, was to guide Billy and his associates throughout the years. The issue of finances would once and for all be resolved when the BGEA was founded, putting the team's work on a sound fiscal footing and rewarding their efforts with salary and benefits commensurate with those achieved by professional church workers.

The Graham organization, unlike many previous evangelistic enterprises, would develop cooperative relationships with local churches and promote both its activities and accomplishments with integrity. As far as sexual impropriety is concerned, Graham and his associates have the highest reputation of moral rectitude.

Charles Riggs   I was an oil field roustabout. I didn't know beans from *whatever,* but God knew that I had a heart to serve him, so it was natural for me to be pulled on board and start working in Billy's ministry. I worked for him for forty-seven years. Billy never one time challenged me on anything that I did; not once did he call me into his office and reprimand me. Once I had won his confidence, I could run the show—*almost.*

We would meet with ministers in a given area to find out if there was enough interest in having Billy Graham come, and we would have our plans in place before he ever arrived. Sometimes we would be in a city months before he got there. Sometimes we had as many as fifteen to twenty thousand people involved in a crusade as choir members, counselors, ushers, or in other tasks. In nearly every crusade we would find new ways to involve more pastors, leaders, and churches.

Henry Holley   We all change but Billy is a great man and a great leader. He has so many wonderful qualities. When he gives one of his associates a responsibility, he knows he can trust them. None of us want to do anything without the integrity and excellence that Billy would demand of us. There is no competition among us; it is just the desire to do the best that we can for the man that we love. When he gave me the assignment to direct the Seoul Crusade [in 1973] I didn't hear from him at all until three days before the meeting. He has the ability of gathering people around him who are competent, and he trusts them. That trust is a wonderful element. I believe that God has called the team around Billy. I think of a verse in 1 Samuel: "And there went from among them a band of men whose heart God had touched" [1 Samuel 10:26].

Millie Dienert   Those times were the highlight of my life because I saw a man behind the scenes who was the very same man that he was behind the pulpit. A crusade that touched my life was one we had in Lubbock, Texas. There, the people in charge of prayer saw to it that everyone involved in the prayer preparation program received the names of all of the students at the local university. These students were prayed for individually before the Crusade. When Mr. Graham gave the invitation, it was just breathtaking to watch droves of young people stand in line to try to get down to the turf to accept Jesus. It was awesome to see God at work because God had been spoken to for such a long time about these young people. The crusades were an evidence of what had been done in prayer preparation.

———————

In his desire to win people to Jesus Christ, in 1949 Graham considered expanding his ministry to include film production. He did so at the suggestion of Dick Ross, a filmmaker who headed Great Commission Films. The following year, Ross made a documentary, in color, based on the Portland Crusade. The evangelist soon established Billy Graham Films, which merged with Ross's company and began operations under the name World Wide Pictures. That company would go on to make many films, which would, in turn, be viewed by millions of people throughout the world.

———————

Bill Brown   I had just graduated from university when I learned that Billy Graham was starting a new film work—I was hired literally right out of college. I was quite pleased because while I always wanted to help spread the Gospel I never felt called to a pulpit ministry. So when this opened up I thought it was a wonderful way to be involved in an outreach without having to preach in a church on Sundays. I began my work with Billy in 1952, handling film distribution for *Mr. Texas*, the first Christian western dramatic film.

Interestingly, a week or two after I started work, I was showing *Mr. Texas* in an auditorium in the Midwest with about two or three thousand people in attendance. At the end of the film, I gave an invitation and 135 people came forward. I thought of the privilege I had, even though I had not been called to preach. I probably had more results in *one meeting* than most ministers had in one year of their church ministry. I was very grateful for that. Wherever we went we had wonderful responses. As in the crusades, we would have counselors and use the same materials, so the films were an extension of Billy's ministry.

The Decision-Making Process

Bill Brown   The decision-making process at World Wide Pictures was primarily done through a board consisting of a group of Christian businessmen who volunteered their services. We would come up with the story ideas and then make the suggestions to the board. Ruth was always very involved—she loved the dramatic aspect—and she was always more than willing to give her opinion. It used to frustrate us a bit in that the board members were not motion picture people.

Billy didn't try to make storywise suggestions, but he would participate—especially through Ruth—in wanting to be certain that the Gospel was in all the films. He pretty much left it up to us. Working for Billy Graham was always a pleasure because he gave you a job to do and let you do it without interfering.

One of the most notable productions by World Wide Pictures is *The Hiding Place,* based on a best-selling book that chronicles the heroic actions of Corrie Ten Boom. Along with nine members of her family, she saved Jews from Nazi persecution during World War II. She and her sister, Betsie, were arrested in their home in the Netherlands and incarcerated in the notorious Ravensbruck concentration camp, where Betsie died.

Bill Brown   It was Ruth who suggested that we could do *The Hiding Place* as a film. It turned out to be what was going to be our most expensive film, with a budget of $1.3 million—we had to do a good deal of location shooting—which was way above what we had spent for any other film. There was much discussion as to whether we should do the film. At first the board said yes, and we did the story line and got way into it. One night, at a Billy Graham team retreat, with several hundred people present, I was sitting next to Corrie [Ten Boom, the real-life heroine of the story] and Billy got up and said that the board had decided the film was too expensive to undertake. Later, I was walking with Corrie back to the hotel where we were staying, and I'll never forget what she said: "Bill, even *Billy Graham* is not God; he doesn't make the final decision. We must just put it in the Lord's hands and trust the Lord that the income will come forth. He owns the cattle on a thousand hills and we must ask that he sell some cattle so we can make that film."

She then received a phone call from a friend who told her that he and his wife had decided to put $50,000 that they had originally designated as a legacy for their daughter (she had been killed in an accident) toward *The Hiding Place*. Yet even this sum did not convince the board to go ahead with the film. One day I was sitting in my office and I thought: there were several million people who had read and loved the book, and if I could find enough of them who would become a family to help pay for the making of the film, maybe we could do it that way. I asked Ruth Graham to draft a letter and I created what I called the "Hiding Place Family." Consequently, forty-four thousand people pledged to give money each month until the film was released. That was the only Billy Graham film that was fully paid for before it was ever released.

Gerald Strober   I met Corrie when I was on assignment for *Parade*. She was one of the most remarkable people I have ever known. While she exuded warmth and had about her the air of a loving aunt, she also possessed a steely inner core, as well as a great passion for people. When I asked her how she and her family had found the courage to defy the Nazis, she replied by quoting Deuteronomy 32:10, a verse that her father had instilled in his children's memory. As Corrie told me, "My father would constantly say 'The Jews are the apple of God's eye.'" It is altogether fitting that Yad Vashem, the memorial to the victims of the Holocaust located in Jerusalem, has honored Corrie by planting a tree in her name on its Avenue of the Righteous Gentiles.

Bill Brown   Up until we made *The Hiding Place,* the films always had Billy Graham in them. Then, because that book had such an impact, it was decided that we could go to doing a non–Billy Graham film. We followed that with the film *Joni,* about a quadriplegic girl whose life did not involve a Billy Graham crusade.

———————

Given Graham's interest in employing a variety of media in spreading the Gospel, he wrote books—twenty-four as of 2003, with another on the way—most of them best-sellers and many of them translated into foreign languages. Back in the 1950s, however, he realized the need for an evangelically oriented magazine that would provide ministers with inspiration as well as practical knowledge of current events. So he established *Christianity Today,* a magazine that if successful would rival *The Christian Century,* the latter a well-regarded publication representing liberal theological concerns.

Graham's initial goal was to mail his biweekly magazine, free of charge, for a two-year period to more than two hundred thousand ministers throughout the nation. In time, the magazine would have a solid subscription base, although for a number of years the BGEA had to help subsidize the publication. Several years following the founding of *Christianity Today,* the Graham organization began publication of *Decision,* a magazine intended for lay readers. It has become the highest-circulating religious publication in the United States.

———————

Roger Palms   He would hire people and let them do their job. Only a couple of times in my twenty-two years as editor of *Decision* did he make a suggestion—and these were only *suggestions.* He'd always follow up with, "But *you're* the editor." He was not a minute-by-minute, hands-on manager. He trusted his people very much.

Bill Brown   I have quite a few letters from Billy in my files. Some of them are pretty critical. If he didn't think something was right, he would tell you. But one after another of them are so complimentary, so kind. He would always find something nice to say; he'd sandwich his complaints between two compliments. It made a big difference; it did make you feel good that you worked for him.

Lane Adams   In the spring of 1970, Billy held a crusade in Knoxville, something I had asked him to do for several years. At the team meeting the morning the Crusade opened, Billy, tongue in cheek, said, "I've asked Lane to bring us a message this morning because he's the only one who seems to know why we're here."

Billy met with me backstage on the opening night of a crusade I held in Asheville, North Carolina. He prayed for me and he said, "Lane, when you come to the invitation, you're going to be the loneliest person on earth. I am going to be the only person here tonight who will understand what you are feeling. Moreover, when you get in the pulpit, you will feel like the wind could blow you over. But by the second or third night you will feel like you have a sword in your hand and you can touch the heart of the last person seated in the last row of the balcony."

On that first night, I was slow in getting to the invitation. When I finally did, I looked down, and there was Billy, seated with Ruth and the children, in the third row. He looked like he had his head between his knees praying for me. Just at that time, I heard the old wooden floors of the convention center begin to creak. I opened my eyes and here came the people responding to the invitation.

The Reverend Dr. Leighton Ford, Graham's brother-in-law; former associate evangelist, BGEA   In January 1949, while I was still a high school student, he came to speak to our youth rally. We knew there would be a great response because of how effective he was in calling people to faith. We thought all of our friends would respond. The auditorium was packed, although it was a very icy, snowy night, and we were very disappointed when there was hardly any response to his altar call. Afterwards, he saw that I was disappointed and he came to the side of the platform, and he put an arm around my shoulder and said, "I believe that God has given you a concern to minister to people, and if you stay humble, God will bless and use you." I remember that arm around my shoulder and the words of encouragement. He didn't reflect on *his own* disappointment; he was thinking about *me.*

Charles Riggs   You just have to believe that all of us in the organization had one desire: to serve and please the Lord and to be responsible for anything that Billy Graham was doing. We never thought we were something special, so our hearts were very much knit together. I had forty-seven wonderful years with Billy Graham. I don't think he ever brought any of us in for discipline. He trusted us to get out there and get that job done. We, of course, wanted to do anything we could to do it right.

Millie Dienert   They all had the same desire; they were together as a team to bring people to know Jesus. They all had a one-track mind, and that was to have the type of program that would tie together the message to do one thing: to bring people to the foot of the cross. It was that very deep bond, a bond of the Spirit, not one that can be built up on its own, that placed them in the same spirit of evangelism.

Lane Adams   I was sitting on the platform next to Billy at a crusade when all of a sudden he turned to me and in dead seriousness he said, "Either Leighton [Ford] or you are better preachers than I am and one of *you* ought to be up here preaching, not *me*." My jaw went slack and I said, "You're joking." He said, "No, I'm *not*." I replied, "What you forget is that you're *Billy Graham,* and who am I? God has gifted you but He has also put a horrific responsibility on you that must be awfully hard to bear at times."

Leighton Ford   A few years ago, when I had been mentoring a group of young Christian leaders, we were meeting in North Carolina and Billy came over and joined us one night. The director of the Billy Graham Center at Wheaton College, who is a very gifted preacher, told me that Billy came up to him and said, "I wish I could spend more time with you; I think you could teach me a lot about how to preach." That's when he [Graham] was way up in his seventies. Billy's strong sense of calling was that it was not so much *his* voice as *God's* voice that he wanted people to hear. I have often heard him say, "If the Lord took his hand off me, my mouth would turn to clay."

Bill Brown   We knew that he was so sincere in what he preached; we would be concerned that our lives reflected that same concern. I can't recall one person who got a divorce while working for him; the team stayed together because we understood the tremendous position that God had given Billy to influence the world for Christ. We felt a part of that. It didn't matter what denominations we were—I don't even know what denominations many of the team members were. I just knew that we were one in purpose desiring to—more than anything else—do the best job possible.

Henry Holley   In 1959 I was stationed at Headquarters Marine Corps, in Washington, D.C., and was involved in preparation for a Billy Graham crusade scheduled for April 1960. I had been involved in the Navigators while in the Marines Corps, and I knew the crusade director, a former Navigator, so he called on me to help him as a part-time volunteer.

After the crusade was over, Dan Piatt and Walter Smyth asked me if I would consider leaving the Marine Corps and joining the BGEA. I had stars in my eyes, that I could be associated with such an organization and was ready to do so. I prayerfully considered it and sought counsel from friends, and everyone thought I should accept. The problem was that I had served seventeen years in the Marine Corps and in another three years I could retire with all my benefits—one person told me that if I left three years short of retirement it would be like a monkey on my back for the rest of my life. I told Dan and Walter that I would wait. By the time I had reached twenty years of service, Vietnam had started, and they were not releasing any Marines.

When I retired from the Marine Corps in 1966, they had a parade for me at Parris Island, South Carolina. The general read my retirement orders and the band marched by and played the Marine Corps Hymn, and then they played "Onward Christian Soldiers" because the general had said that I was going to join the Billy Graham team. That was quite a surprise. Walter Smyth, the vice president of the BGEA, was in the stands and when the general bade me Godspeed and I saluted and did an about-face, Walter extended his hand and said, "Welcome aboard." That was my transition from the Marine Corps to the Billy Graham Evangelistic Association. Ten days later, I was preparing a crusade in Tokyo.

Bill Brown   I was the first team member to take my family on the road. We would go to a city for eight to ten months—we moved once when our baby was four days old—and by the time my son, Bill, was fourteen he had had twenty-two different homes. It was hard on Joan; she had the choice of having a permanent home or traveling as a family, and she preferred to be together. She would wonder if every city we would go to would be the last one. But then she would go to the crusade and see one invitation and see the people coming forward, and she'd say, "OK, Lord, I'll do *another*."

Millie Dienert   When we [the Graham and Dienert families] were on any vacation together, it was what somebody else would call "working time." We always prayed together; we prayed for renewed vision for the ministry. It wasn't a time of fun and games; it was a time of refreshment to our bodies and a time we prayed for our families, and for the ministry and what could be done to enlarge the ministry so that more people would come to know the Lord. That was the desire of his heart on vacation. He had one desire; the man was consumed with the desire to win people to Jesus Christ. The men would chat back and forth and share and prepare for the next crusade. It was a time of working together in prayer and thought.

Chapter Four

FROM HARRINGAY ARENA TO MADISON SQUARE GARDEN

As a result of the huge boost given his ministry by both the success in Los Angeles and the immediate, positive, response to "The Hour of Decision," Graham began to receive invitations to hold meetings in many American cities. From 1951 to 1953, he conducted crusades in southern cities, including Shreveport, Memphis, Greensboro, Raleigh, Jackson, Chattanooga, and Asheville; in the southwest in Dallas, Fort Worth, Houston, Albuquerque, and West Texas; and in Cincinnati, St. Louis, Washington, D.C., Pittsburgh, Syracuse, and Detroit.

While in Washington in early 1952, Graham was visited by two Christian leaders from Britain who raised the possibility of his holding a crusade in London. In March, he spoke to a gathering of hundreds of British clergymen at Church House, Westminster. Later that year, a delegation representing the Evangelical Alliance came to Asheville with an invitation for Billy to hold a crusade in London beginning on March 1, 1954. The first items on the Crusade's planning agenda concerned its venue and budget, the then-unheard-of sum of $50,000 for publicity *alone*.

Seeking a Venue for the London Crusade

Maurice Rowlandson   I was given the task of looking at various possible venues, but nothing seemed suitable. In the end, it was decided to import an aluminum tabernacle built by the U.S. industrialist R. G. Le

Tourneau. We had received permission to erect it in the Wembley Stadium car park. Two Englishmen were sent over to see it, but when they arrived in America they learned that the aluminum tabernacle had collapsed. The only location we could find that was accessible for an extended period was the Harringay Arena.

Harringay

Maurice Rowlandson   There was no support from the official church. The Evangelical Alliance formed a special committee to work on the meetings. It is interesting to note that the committee never took a vote; there was always a unanimous feeling about the effort. The only controversy involved a calendar that was produced at Graham headquarters in Minneapolis. One entry stated that in Britain whatever Hitler's bombs failed to do, socialism soon achieved. That phrase raised a furor in the House of Commons, where questions were asked [concerning] whether this American evangelist ever should be allowed to land. It was thought that he was a political rather than a religious animal. But someone pointed out that the word "socialism" was spelled with a small *s*; it was not the capital *S* of the Labor Party. And that won the day. But, of course, that controversy got us an incredible wealth of publicity.

The curiosity value started by the publicity was the factor that really won the battle in getting the crowds. This was largely the inspiration of Jerry Beavan, who got the buses to carry placards on their sides featuring Billy's face and advertising the Crusade.

Joan Winmill Brown, actress, author, counseled by Ruth Graham at London Crusade, 1954   I had seen the advertising on the buses that Billy was in town and had heard about him on the radio. I thought I would love to go and hear what this American had to say about the Lord. I was at a low point in my life; I was contemplating suicide, and I cried out to the Lord, "Please, help me." It was just after that that the phone rang; a friend was inviting me to go to the Crusade. I went with about six people. As I look back, it is just so wonderful how the Lord answered that prayer.

The timing of the Harringay Crusade was propitious, occurring just two years following the coming to the British throne of Queen Elizabeth II, a young and beautiful monarch. Her accession appeared to augur a "new Elizabethan age," and it coincided with a major development in Britain: the end of post–World War II austerity. Now the lives of a courageous people who had struggled daily merely to subsist were easing, and they were ready to examine issues related to their spiritual lives.

The First Evening

Although a huge publicity campaign had been mounted—it won two awards in the United Kingdom—Graham fretted about the possibility of failure. He was concerned as to whether, if people *did* come out, they would respond well to his preaching style. Early on the evening of the opening session, March 1, 1954, he waited in his hotel room for Beavan to give him a reading on the size of the crowd; the initial numbers were not promising. Now, more than fifty years later, Beavan believes that Graham's and other team members' recollections concerning opening night attendance are not accurate.

Gerald Beavan I called Billy about half an hour before the meeting was to start and I told him there were not many people here yet. People were coming out on the tubes [London subway] and they hadn't gotten there yet. There was no prophecy of doom; it was just a simple statement of fact. By the time Billy got there, the place was filled. And it was filled every night.

Maurice Rowlandson At about 6:00 P.M., Jerry Beavan phoned Billy Graham at his hotel to tell him that hardly anyone had showed up at Harringay. When Billy arrived about an hour or so later, he was a bit worried because he found no crowd standing outside waiting to get in. But he was on the wrong end; the crowds were all at the *other* end.

The Invitation: A Question of Style

Maurice Rowlandson Billy was advised by some people not to give an invitation. On the first night, and on the first night only, he gave an American-style invitation. He said, "All heads bowed, all eyes closed, and put your hand up if you want to come to Christ." When that was over, he asked those who had raised their hands to come to the front. That was not the sort of invitation the Brits went for. That night the British evangelist Tom Rees met with Billy and talked to him about the kind of invitation that he would like to see. From the second night onward, Billy used the straight forward, "I want you to get out of your seat and come to the front."

Joan Winmill Brown   Billy preached on the verse "Seek ye first the kingdom of God; and His Righteousness; and all these things shall be added unto you" [Matthew 6: 33], and I realized that as an actress I had been seeking *my* kingdom and I had put God to the side. As a child, I had had a wonderful Christian teacher who had led me to love the Lord, but I felt that to be an actress you had to put all that aside. I also remember Billy saying, "If *you* were the only person in the world, Christ would have died for you." That really hit me because I thought: Christ died for the sins of the world, not just for *me*. I had always loved the Lord, but I had never known what it was to have a personal Savior. When I went down, I thought: I'm not taking my life; I'm going to give it all to the Lord.

––––––––––––

Although the London Crusade would not produce the sensational conversions that occurred during the Los Angeles meeting, the British people were impressed, cumulatively, by the steady stream of inquirers coming forward at his invitation each evening. By the end of the twelve-week run, more than thirty-six thousand of the two million attendees made decisions and received counseling.

––––––––––––

Joan Winmill Brown   I was taken to the counseling room, and I was led to Ruth [Graham]. Unbeknownst to me, one of the people in my party who thought this was going to ruin my career had run into Jerry Beavan, and that's how I got to see Ruth. When I looked into her eyes, I immediately saw that peace that I had so long wanted to find in my own life. Afterwards she asked me if I would like to meet her husband. I said, "Well, yes," but I really didn't want to; I didn't even know who she was. Then she knocked on the door and the door opened and there was Billy. I was just so shattered that it was *him*.

I was so shocked that I was actually meeting him. And he was so excited when Ruth told him that I had come to the Lord, and he said how wonderful it was. All I could say was "yes" and "no." Later, he said to Ruth, "Do you think you really got through to the girl?" Of course, Ruth followed me up so wonderfully. When I came home that evening, some of my actor friends insisted that nothing had happened. I was feeling quite dejected, and then I saw that there was a parcel waiting for me. Ruth had sent me *Peace with God*. I sat up that night reading it. To me it is one of the most wonderful books because it really tells so simply of the great need in our lives and how we can find that peace that passes all understanding. When I woke up in the morning, I was still holding that book. I had the assurance that the Lord really loved me and that he had forgiven me for all the sins in my life.

People living far from London did not even have to travel to Harringay Arena to hear Graham's message. With assistance from an American radio engineer who devised a system of broadcasting by telephone using World War II-era landline relays, people who were gathered in churches and rented halls in more than 170 cities throughout the United Kingdom were able to listen to Crusade sessions.

On the Crusade's final day, as a drenching rain fell, Graham spoke to an audience of sixty thousand at White City Stadium. That evening, as the pelting rain continued, 110,000 people—the largest crowd to gather there to that date—made their way to Wembley Stadium. As the huge throng began to assemble, Maurice Rowlandson, who had organized a shuttle to bring the choir members, counselors, and ushers there from White City, asked the stadium's manager to give unprecedented approval for the overflow to stand on the field. Telephoning his superior, the manager was told that he could allow one hundred people onto the field. Within a matter of minutes, *ten thousand* would make their way onto the rain-soaked turf.

At the end of the service, Dr. Geoffrey Fisher, the Archbishop of Canterbury, observed to Grady Wilson, "We may never see a sight like that this side of Heaven." Caught up in the emotion of the moment, Grady threw his arms around the prelate, exclaiming, "That's right, Brother Archbishop!" Years later, Grady would tell of an Anglican archbishop who questioned why the team had traveled to Britain on an ocean liner, whereas Jesus had entered Jerusalem on a donkey. "Well," the irrepressible Grady replied, "I don't think our Lord could have crossed the Atlantic on an ass."

The Impact of Harringay

Gerald Beavan   Prior to London, most crusades lasted four or perhaps six weeks. We felt that long crusades are necessary to have an impact upon a community. As far as London was concerned, we couldn't have touched that vast city in three or four weeks. We stayed there twelve weeks.

In retrospect, Harringay was the major turning point, probably the most important single event in Billy's career. Up until then he had been an itinerant evangelist moving across America, essentially in the South, having meetings in the largest available building. Harringay marked a complete departure: it was in a foreign country, in a foreign environment, and proved that this same message and this same method could be effective anywhere in the world—that it was not just confined to the Bible Belt of America. And those twelve weeks in London changed him from being an itinerant American evangelist to a world evangelist. He was never the same after that. I don't think the importance of Harringay has ever been clearly delineated.

Maurice Rowlandson   By the end of the twelve weeks, many of the counselors were people who had themselves responded to the invitation at the beginning of the Crusade. The long-term impact is such that there are a great many people today who look back to the Harringay days as the time they started their lives as Christians. Many vicars, rectors, and one or two bishops were converted through Billy Graham's 1954 Crusade.

William Martin   Certainly there are people outside the churches who feel very positively toward Billy Graham. This has to do with shared values, although they didn't get these values from Graham. In places like England, it is said that much of the evangelical growth now comes from people—and the descendants of people—who were converted at Harringay in 1954. That has had an impact on the churches, and obviously on the society. But gauging the social impact is a tricky business.

Post-Harringay

Maurice Rowlandson   Many people believe that if Billy Graham had continued, the whole experience could have swept across the British Isles. Part of the reason this didn't happen was due to the advice of the Archbishop of Canterbury [Dr. Geoffrey Fisher], who felt that Billy should go and let the churches get on with it and build on what Graham had started. And, of course, Billy was very, very tired after the twelve weeks. I myself was at Harringay from 2:00 P.M. to midnight every day for twelve weeks.

Gerald Beavan   Immediately after Harringay, we went to [the continent of] Europe, where Billy began speaking through an interpreter. He used the unique method of speaking sentence by sentence, phrase by phrase, rather than in paragraphs. We conveyed that message to President Kennedy, and he adopted that technique when speaking overseas. We came to New York and stayed sixteen weeks. We went to Australia and stayed for two months. We used to speak of short-duration crusades as "hit and run evangelism." We weren't engaged in this kind of evangelism, but rather in saturation evangelism. That is how we made an impact.

Anna-Lisa Madeira   It's wonderful how he has become respected by the whole world. When he first was on the docket, the press here and in England was terrible; they were sure he was another Elmer Gantry. Today there is nobody who doesn't respect him. His life has been so free from blemish and so very honest.

An Unanticipated Dividend of Harringay

Joan Winmill Brown   About a year after I came forward at Harringay, the Graham organization asked me to appear in a film called *Souls in Conflict*. I was invited to speak at the premiere at Carnegie Hall. Bill [Brown] was working in film distribution for the Graham organization, and he was sent to meet me at the airport, and that's how it all began. We had our fiftieth anniversary in April 2005. It's amazing how the film continues to be used.

Looking back, the Lord was working even when I became an actress; He knew one day I would have a ministry that way with Him. The director of the film, Dick Ross, a very dedicated Christian, was wonderful. He would come up and whisper comments, rather than shouting out, as might other directors. I was also working with Colleen Townsend Evans, who was a wonderful American actress. She helped me so much; we had prayer together every morning. I would always see her with her Bible; it taught me how much the Word should mean in our lives. My love for the Word really began there.

Madison Square Garden

After spending the better part of 1955 on a return visit to Britain and a tour of the European continent, as well as most of 1956 in India and the Far East, Graham began to prepare for his greatest challenge to date: a crusade in New York's

Madison Square Garden. Officially sponsored by the Protestant Council of New York City, it would begin on May 15 and was originally scheduled to conclude on June 30.

Lane Adams   In February 1957, Billy called a team meeting at the Laymen's House in Rye, New York, where one of the rules was that you must sign up for some work activity to earn your keep. I signed up to pick up frozen, rotten apples in the apple orchard—as had Billy. In our first meeting, he asked me some questions about my days as a Navy fighter pilot. He said, "The New York Crusade is the largest undertaking we've ever had, and this will be the largest team we've ever had." He asked if I had any suggestions and I replied that, given the number of people involved, he needed someone who knew their abilities and could coordinate their efforts. He then asked who on the team would be the person to perform this responsibility. I said that the best person was Billy's brother-in-law, Leighton Ford, and Leighton took over coordination of the team.

Leighton Ford   I was the director of ministerial relations. My responsibility was to go to New York ahead of time to meet with groups of clergy and with individual congregations and to explain the crusade, motivate them, and recruit them, and at Billy's request my wife and I moved to New York in the fall of 1956. Later, I was in charge of a group of twelve to fifteen associate evangelists who spoke all through the New York area. When Billy asked me to go up there, I was twenty-four years old and had just finished seminary the year before. Looking back, I wonder: if that had been *me,* would *I* have put a man of that age in charge of that aspect of my work? And although he knew me personally, he was taking a pretty big risk because this was the largest crusade he had ever done.

To organize this prodigious event, Graham again called on Beavan. Four months before the Crusade was to begin, however, Beavan, citing personal reasons, resigned from the BGEA. Billy was not sure who should replace him.

Leighton Ford   He took a chance with Charlie Riggs, who took over as director of the Crusade when Jerry Beavan had to step aside, although Charlie had never directed a crusade before.

Charles Riggs   When the person who was directing the Madison Square Garden Crusade had to leave his post, Billy wanted someone else to take over. But Roger Hull, the lay chairman of the Crusade's executive committee, insisted, "Charlie's our man."

Hull, who was the executive vice president of Mutual Life Insurance of New York and chairman of the Crusade's executive committee, recommended Charles Riggs. Hull, who had been impressed not only by Riggs's professional abilities but also by his spiritual nature, told Graham, "If anything happens in New York for God, it's got to be by prayer. And Charlie Riggs is a man of prayer."

Lane Adams   A couple of days into the retreat, Leighton Ford asked me what I thought of Billy. I replied, "Billy is a combination of the wisdom of Solomon and the enthusiasm of a twelve-year-old boy about to go fishing with his Daddy." I have never backed off that description except to add one thing: "Behold an Israelite in whom there is no guile."

Leighton Ford   He takes much time every day to read his Bible and to pray. In team meetings during crusades, Billy would pray with the same fervency with which he would preach. It was very intense; you had the sense that he really believed that he was talking to someone greater than himself. At the retreat before the opening of the Madison Square Garden Crusade, Ralph Mitchell preached at the Sunday morning worship service and told of a pastor who drew a circle on the floor. He knelt down in the circle and asked the Lord to start a revival within that circle. Someone saw the pastor and asked him what he was doing and the pastor said, "Come on down; there's room for you." And Ralph said that is what we all ought to pray, and *he* said, "Come on down; there's room for you." Before anyone could move, Billy came down from the back row, where he was sitting, and knelt at the front. For some people that would have been just a display, but for Billy it was the genuine hunger of his heart to be very real before God. That is what I tell young leaders: prayer is really the real self coming before the real God.

Arthur Bailey   America had heard about Billy Graham in 1949 as a result of the Los Angeles Crusade, but it was in the sixteen-week Madison Square Garden Crusade in 1957 that America saw him *in person,* through television. The 1957 Crusade was a phenomenon that took evangelism to a new level and introduced Mr. Graham to a world audience.

That world audience included influential critics close to home, among them Dr. Reinhold Niebuhr, the Missouri-born theologian who was the pastor of a Detroit church during the Depression before arriving at the Union Theological Seminary, located at Broadway and 122nd Street, just a few miles north of the Garden. He had published an article in *Life* magazine questioning Graham's promise to new believers of a new life in Christ by "merely signing a decision card." To Niebuhr, Graham's message was "too simple in any age, but particularly so in a nuclear one with its great moral perplexities." Stung by criticism from a theologian of Niebuhr's stature, Graham asked George Champion, an influential New Yorker and a member of the Crusade's executive committee, to arrange an appointment for him with Niebuhr. Niebuhr, however, would not meet with Billy.

Leighton Ford   Niebuhr thought that his theology was too pietistic, too individualistic, with not enough emphasis on corporate sin.

Lane Adams   During the retreat he held prior to the New York Crusade, he was reminded by members of the team that some of the people who had first supported him were turning against him because of some of the people he had welcomed into the Crusade's support group. These critics were saying terrible things about Billy, and one or two of the team members who had been with him for years urged Billy to answer his critics. I will never forget his response: "No!" And he named these men, all of whom were getting older, and said, "The word of God says 'Touch not God's anointed' and history has shown that these men are God's anointed. If they are right, God will not bless us; if our approach is right, He will bless us. I am not going to answer the critics or be critical of them."

Leighton Ford   Some people were dubious, even hypercritical, that Billy would associate with the Council of Churches—that he would be with people they considered "liberal." In effect, Billy was saying, I welcome anybody to this platform who will support what we're doing, even if they don't completely agree with my theology or me with *theirs*. I think the criticisms hurt Billy very much. He had to learn to make his way through criticism from both sides.

Ben Armstrong   He had preached in various places in the world. But here he was, in New York City, the most important city in terms of radio because that's where the networks are and because there were the great theologians. He had heard about Dr. Paul Tillich and Dr. Reinhold Niebuhr, who were professors at Union Theological Seminary. He wanted to see Dr. Niebuhr but wasn't able to. I didn't realize he wanted to see Niebuhr; otherwise I probably could have done something. I was a student of Niebuhr and as one of his graduate students I could have very easily gotten Billy an appointment. While Billy was never able to meet Niebuhr, he had fantastic success with many churches in New York.

Reinhold Niebuhr never accepted Billy Graham. He told me that Billy was too simple in his approach. He thought Billy was a good man, but he said that Billy could never be effective because he did not have a real understanding of the dynamic forces in religion and in modern society. Niebuhr was filled up with his own studies, with his status as the number one theologian in the nation, and just didn't pay much attention to Billy Graham. Billy reached the ordinary man on the street. The average person was very impressed by his approach and very responsive. The people I knew in my studies at New York University and at Columbia weren't paying any attention to him.

Gerald Beavan   There had been much talk about coming to New York, particularly after London. In 1955, I began meeting with Dan Potter, who was head of the Protestant Council in the City of New York. I opened an office in 1956. The Presbyterians were not completely on board, and we had a meeting involving them. This one man said that the problem he saw with Billy Graham was that he had no social acceptability. Another Presbyterian minister, who had come from Scotland, said, "That's a very interesting phrase. I see Billy meeting with our prime minister, Mr. Churchill; I see him meeting with my Queen; I see pictures of him meeting with President Eisenhower; and with Vice President Nixon. So tell me, what is your standard of social acceptability?" That carried the day. Pretty soon we had a very united effort, except that the extreme fundamentalists never participated in the New York Crusade.

———————

The criticism hurled at Graham from some fundamentalist leaders hurt more than did charges directed at him from liberals. Men such as Bob Jones Sr., Carl McIntire, and eventually John R. Rice railed against Graham's practice of inclusion—what his long-time associate Robert Ferm termed "cooperative evan-gelism." Those fundamentalist leaders, who continued to represent large con-stituencies, attacked Graham in language less genteel than that employed by Niebuhr. To them, Graham had sold out—all the more so by coming to New York at the invitation of an organization whose membership included churchmen who did not believe in fundamentals of faith, such as the inspiration of the Scripture, the Virgin Birth, and in some extreme instances the bodily resurrection of Christ.

William Martin   He broke with the fundamentalists in New York in 1957. At past crusades I have attended, I have seen him picketed, as in New York in 2005. The people who picket are not Unitarians; they're fundamentalists. You can go to Websites where Billy Graham is attacked for selling out to the devil.

In a dairy entry on May 9, just days before the opening of the Crusade, Graham wrote:

> During the past few months we have faced many obstacles and problems. I guess I have been on the phone to New York an average of three or four times a day. Many problems seemed to be impossible to solve, and yet somehow they have been solved. It seems a few months ago that opposition from the extreme liberals and the extreme fundamentalists would combine to put a hurdle in the pathway of blessing. Most of this opposition has now dissipated, I believe, in answer to prayer. . . . Gradually the Spirit of God shed abroad in my heart an overwhelming love for these brethren whom I believe to be tragically mistaken. I have thanked God a thousand times in the last few days that He gave me grace, during these months of severe attacks, never to answer back [quoted in *God in the Garden,* by Curtis Mitchell].

On opening night, as Graham waited to deliver his sermon, he silently prayed: "What I said would glorify God as it went out to the whole world." In *God in the Garden,* Mitchell quotes Graham's diary entry: "Waiting to ascend the podium, I still did not feel great liberty in my soul and that great abandonment that I love to feel when I preach. I looked down and saw Carl Henry, editor of *Christianity Today,* and just as I saw him, he bowed his head in prayer. This seemed repre-sentative of thought throughout the world. Suddenly, a great surge of joy swept my soul that brought tears to my eyes. When I stepped to the platform I knew that God was going to speak through me."

In addition to opposition from the theological left and right, Graham grappled with the issue of why his Garden audiences were overwhelmingly white, despite the support of such highly prestigious African American pastors as Gardner Taylor, the pastor of Brooklyn's Concord Baptist Church; and M. L. Wilson, of the Convent Avenue Baptist Church in Manhattan. As a southerner who had come to abhor segregation, Graham may have felt a special urgency to reach out to New York City's large black community. So important was the question to him that he asked a friend in New York to recommend an African American evangelist who could join the crusade team.

Howard Jones   My wife, Wanda, and I had just returned home from a two-month tour of West Africa, where I had held crusades. There was a letter from my friend Jack Wyrtzen. He wrote that he had had breakfast with Billy Graham in New York, where Billy was holding a crusade at Madison Square Garden. Jack found Billy quite discouraged because even though he was preaching to thousands of people each evening, he was not reaching people of color. He told Jack that he and the team were praying for wisdom and then asked Jack if he knew an African American evangelist. Jack replied, "Yes, I have your man; his name is Howard Jones."

In his letter Jack said that he knew I was tired but he asked me to get to New York as soon as possible. The next day, Wanda and I flew to New York, and when the Crusade service ended Billy came up to us and gave us a great big bear hug and said, "Hello, Howard and Wanda. God bless you, my brother and my sister." And he told of the burden in his heart concerning the absence of people of color in his audiences. He asked, "Could you come and help me?"

Billy asked me how he could attract people of color to the Garden. I said, "If they're not coming, go where they are." He asked what I meant, and I replied, "Go to Harlem." When the news broke that Billy had added an African American evangelist to his team, there was a strong reaction from some white pastors in New York City and the surrounding area. Soon Billy was receiving letters and telephone calls saying: "You don't need that 'N' preacher on your team and if you keep Howard Jones, we will not support you anymore." Some white pastors warned Billy not to go to Harlem, telling him those "savages" would kill him.

I picked up Billy, Bev, and Cliff in a taxi and we headed to the Salem Methodist Church. On our way, it started to rain and Billy wondered if anyone would show up since the rally was planned for outdoors. When we arrived, my heart sank; all the seats were empty. We walked up the steps of the church and were met by the pastor, who exclaimed, "Howard we have four to five thousand people packed into the church!" Just then, a deacon came running up to tell us that the sun was shining, so we went outside and Billy preached to a crowd of eight thousand people, with others listening from nearby brownstone apartment windows. He said, "I came to you and now I want you to come to the Garden. You're all invited."

The next Sunday we went to Brooklyn, where Billy preached to ten thousand people. That night, Cliff asked Ethel Waters to come down from the choir to the podium, where her rendition of "His Eye Is on the Sparrow" brought down the house. From then on, we had a Crusade that was colored—colored with whites and different people of color. It was a miracle.

Lois K. Akehurst, attendee, Madison Square Garden Crusade, 1957; wife of Rev. William Akehurst of the BGEA   I was eighteen years old. A friend asked me to join her at the Madison Square Garden Crusade. She had started to open the Scriptures up, telling me how Jesus died for me. Although this made me very uncomfortable, I went to the Garden. I have kept the ticket from that evening all these years because it was the day of my salvation. I enjoyed everything about the experience of being in Madison Square Garden that evening. I heard Ethel Waters and George Beverly Shea sing, and as I listened to Dr. Graham, he touched something inside of me. When he asked: "Have you made a decision for the Lord Jesus Christ"? I knew that I had not done that. I knew that I had to go forward, and so I ran forward. When I arrived in front of the platform, there was a counselor waiting for me and we prayed together.

The initial six-week meeting stretched to sixteen, including a service at Yankee Stadium attracting 100,000—a record crowd for that venerable arena. The final Crusade statistics would be staggering: a total attendance of 2.3 million, of whom more than 56,000 made decisions, while the final budget exceeded $2.5 million, a first for a Graham crusade. Another milestone was achieved when Shea, "America's beloved Gospel singer," sang his now-classic composition "How Great Thou Art."

The marathon meeting tested both Graham's ability to come up with fresh sermon material and his physical strength. On some evenings, he would experience "liberty and power" as he presented his message, while on others he "sensed the greatest spiritual power." He would write in his diary, "Never in my ministry have I sensed the presence of God in any place as I have in Madison Square Garden. . . . I do not ever remember having had such complete abandonment and freedom of spirit."

In *Just As I Am*, Graham expanded on his great responsibility when preaching the Gospel: "From that moment I stand up to speak to a crowd, I am thinking of that person whose life is being crushed by heartache or alcohol or family problems and I want to make the hope of the Gospel as clear as possible to him or to her. . . . Preaching also involves us in a spiritual battle with the forces of evil. I am always deeply conscious that I am absolutely helpless and that only the Holy Spirit can penetrate the minds and hearts of those who are without Christ."

A more secular evaluation of Billy's preaching was made by Whitney Bolton, a reporter with the New York *Telegraph,* who wrote, "He is like an excellent salesman: he describes the goods in plain terms, lets you see them and decide on them. He avoids the old, ranting ways and the pulpit thumping. He is a skilled and wise and practiced salesman of a commodity he truly believes should be in every home."

As the days turned into weeks, the lengthy Crusade was proving to be exhausting to the Graham team, a situation Billy sought to remedy for one devoted associate.

––––––––––

Lane Adams   On Sunday night, at the Garden, Billy looked at me as we sat on the platform and remarked, "You look tired." I said, "Billy we are *all* tired, *you especially,* since you have to preach every night." He said, "Do you have anything on your schedule for tomorrow that can't be canceled?" I replied, "No, I don't." So he told me to go to my apartment and to put together some casual clothes and a shaving kit and meet him at the Garden after the meeting ended. When I arrived back at the Garden, there was a large limousine waiting to take me, Billy, Ruth, and Grady [Wilson] to the home of a publisher. On the way, Billy told me that on the door of my bedroom I would find a little black button on the jam, and he said, "When you wake up tomorrow morning, get out of bed, push that button, jump back in bed, and see what happens." The next morning, I followed Billy's instructions. After about ten minutes, there was a knock on the door and in came a butler with a full, beautiful breakfast tray. Later that day, Billy asked if I had mashed that button. When I said that I had, he laughed. What impressed me was that he had noticed that one of his team members was fatigued and needed rest.

The Crusade provided an opportunity for some of Graham's friends from Wheaton College to see him in action on a much larger stage than that of the Tab or the Western Springs Baptist Church. Interestingly, those friends did not attempt to meet with him, realizing perhaps that the demands on his time were already enormous. For example, Joyce and Don Mostrom were happy just to be a part of the great enterprise, although Joyce regrets to this day not having invited the Grahams to their home for dinner.

Joyce Mostrom   In the 1950s, Don and I lived in Jersey City. Both of us participated in the Madison Square Garden Crusade as counselors. It was exciting to be part of a large effort. We took a course in preparation and were part of this huge crowd of people who were going to be counselors. It was a wonderful time to be part of all that God was doing, to hear the marvelous music, and the straight Gospel message. He clearly presented the Gospel; he didn't try to dress it up. It was sort of *in your face.*

Anna-Lisa Madeira   It was wonderful to be there, to sense the spirit and to sense the way people were being reached. At first we didn't think of it as anything momentous; it became that as the summer wore on. You couldn't help but think back to the days when we would say, "He is going to go places." You knew that there was something extraordinary about him and that God was going to use him wonderfully. We could have no imagination how God was going to use him. But I think all students sensed something very special about him and about Ruth too; you just knew they were different from everybody else while being very comfortable with everybody else.

One of Graham's greatest concerns in appearing in New York, the nation's media capital, was how he would be treated there. His fear was somewhat eased when the *New York Journal American,* a Hearst newspaper, carried a sympathetic, five-part series written by the nationally syndicated columnist Dorothy Kilgallen. On the eve of the Crusade's opening, Billy was interviewed by national television anchors Walter Cronkite and Dave Garroway, as well as by a number of local radio personalities. Then, during the crusade, such major publications as *Life, Look,* and *Ebony* assigned photographers and ran feature articles.

Ben Armstrong   The media was very kind to Billy Graham. Some people would say that the media *made* Billy Graham. Billy understood what Marshall McLuhan had written about—that radio was a hot medium but television was a cool medium. The decision to go on television live every Saturday night was a major victory for Billy. In New York, Billy was able to meet the presidents of NBC and CBS and, because of his persuasiveness, was able to secure time.

Martin Luther King Jr. Attends the Crusade

In a further attempt to win black support and broaden his New York base, Graham took the unusual step of inviting the rising civil rights leader Dr. Martin Luther King Jr. to sit with him on the platform and offer a prayer.

Howard Jones   One day, Billy told me that he planned to invite Martin Luther King Jr. to the Crusade. He added that we should be prepared for strong resistance if Martin came. On the first night that Martin was there, Billy asked him to lead in prayer. As Martin walked to the podium, a group of people began to jeer. But when that man began to pray, he took us to heaven. It was a marvelous prayer and when he finished thousands of people stood on their feet and clapped and clapped.

That evening, after the service, Billy held a dinner for Martin to which I and other team members were invited. Billy asked Martin how he had managed to pull off the Montgomery [Alabama] bus boycott without violence or bloodshed. Martin was a very interesting man. If you asked him a question, he would never respond quickly. He would drop his head and go into a meditative mood. When he did answer he told us that he and a group of pastors had prayed, asking the Holy Spirit for a plan. And that plan was a bus boycott.

Gerald Beavan   We met Dr. King when we were going with him to Rio for a meeting of the Baptist World Alliance. We flew on Pan American in a DC-7 and lost an engine and had to set down in Kingston, Jamaica, and stay overnight in a hotel. The Pan Am representative there informed me that only three rooms, with two beds apiece, were available. We decided that Charlie Riggs [a BGEA staff member] and I would stay in one room, that Billy would have a room to himself, and that Grady [Wilson] would stay in the third room. Billy insisted that Dr. King share the room with Grady. The next morning we were having breakfast and Dr. King came down and put his hand on Grady and said, "Good morning, roommate." Grady, of course, was a devout southerner, and for the two or three days we were in Rio whenever Martin Luther King would see Grady he'd call out, "Hey, roomie!" That became a family joke.

Howard Jones   Many people assumed that Billy and Martin were enemies; but that's wrong. They were friends, *good* friends. Billy told me that he and Martin would often exchange birthday greetings. Martin would often say to Billy, "I'm proud of the fact that you are holding integrated crusades. I want you to know that what you are doing now with these integrated crusades is helping me in my work."

William Martin   He has played a role, better than many people recognize, in telling evangelicals that it was wrong to be racist and segregationist.

Leighton Ford   I don't think they were close friends in terms of knowing each other really well. But certainly they had a great deal of respect for each other. For Billy to have Martin Luther King on the platform in New York was politically a good thing although it was dangerous, as it was to have some of these Council of Churches people there. But it was also a genuine appreciation that Martin Luther King had been called to do something important that was not Billy's calling. I was told by the president of Bell Haven University in Jackson, Mississippi, that they are buying the football stadium where Billy preached in the early 1950s. It is his plan to put up a plaque to remember the day that Billy pulled down the ropes that divided the white and black areas.

Gerald Beavan   Billy did make some strides in breaking the old segregation barrier in the South. In New Orleans, I was instructed by Billy that there be no segregation in the stadium meetings. When I presented that ultimatum to the local executive committee, I told them there would be no black section. One member, who was violently opposed to this, came forward one night and was wonderfully saved and became a different person. We did the same thing in Little Rock when there was an issue over school integration. Billy used to say that there was no color line at the foot of the cross.

––––––––––––

If Los Angeles put Billy on the national map and London made him an international personality, New York catapulted him to new heights. For better or for worse—and with all the responsibilities inherent in his new stature—Billy would become *the* face of evangelism. In achieving his unprecedented success at the Garden, he had bested the old-time fundamentalists, making *his* brand of evangelicalism the one that would, by the turn of the twentieth century, be practiced by more than thirty million Americans.

––––––––––––

William Martin   They saw that they were losing, that nobody wanted the older fundamentalism any more. I'd like to think they were reading their Bible and had decided the older fundamentalism was not the spirit of Jesus, not the spirit of the prophets—that it is now time to reach out rather than draw the circle tight.

––––––––––––

In the years from the conclusion of his Madison Square Garden Crusade in September 1957 to his visit to Moscow in 1982, Graham would conduct crusades and meetings in more than two hundred cities, including many in the United States and throughout the world: Belfast, Brussels, Cairo, Copenhagen, Glasgow, Hamburg, Johannesburg, Manila, Mexico City, Prague, Rio de Janeiro, Singapore, Sydney, Taipei, Tokyo, Toronto, Turin, Wellington, Zagreb. Additionally, his schedule was filled with meetings with business, political, and religious leaders, as well as with media interviews and appearances at conferences and on college and university campuses.

Although his ministry was largely consumed with the winning of souls, he was also vitally interested in the future of evangelism, as well as in the preparation of workers to carry out the Great Commission. Graham's concerns in the latter area led to the BGEA's sponsorship of several international meetings, beginning in 1966 in Berlin. There, seven hundred delegates and two hundred observers, along with one hundred representatives of the media, joined in a World Congress on Evangelism intended to be the spiritual successor to a world missionary conference that was held in Edinburgh in 1910. The theme of the Berlin meeting was "one race, one gospel, one task," and its purpose was "to establish evangelism's relevance to the modern world, to underline its urgency, to explore new forms of witness, and to show the world that God is in truth Lord of all, and that he saves men through His Son."

On the basis of the success of the Berlin Congress, Graham and his associates in 1974 organized an International Congress on World Evangelism, held from July 16 to 25 at the Palais de Beaulieu, in Lausanne, Switzerland; the theme was "Let the earth hear his voice." Four thousand delegates from 150 nations were drawn to the congress, where a document, the Lausanne Covenant, was issued. It contained the clause: "The message of salvation implies also a message of judgment upon every form of alienation, oppression and discrimination and we should not be afraid to denounce evil and injustice wherever they exist."

Ben Armstrong   It was the most important international conference Billy had. I was there to head up the radio and television effort. We set up interviews with major networks, including BBC, German television, and French television. Billy and other leaders were available for interviews each day.

Leighton Ford   The Lausanne Conference was certainly a watershed in terms of the new evangelicalism internationally. I believe no one but Billy could have brought together the delegates from around the world. I think the legacy of the Lausanne movement—of which I was the follow-up chairman for many years—will be one of Billy's real legacies.

Graham's concern for the training of evangelists, particularly those from developing nations, would lead to the organization in 1983 in Amsterdam of an International Conference for Itinerant Evangelists, characterized by one of his associates as an effort to "reach the guys out in the bushes." That meeting attracted thirty-nine hundred delegates; from its success, three years later the BGEA would organize a similar event for nine thousand invited participants.

Then in 2000, at Graham's invitation, ten thousand evangelists, mission strategists, church leaders, and theologians from more than two hundred countries met in Amsterdam to "pray, worship, and discern the wisdom of the Holy Spirit for the unfinished task of world evangelism." At the conclusion of their deliberations, the delegates adopted the Amsterdam Declaration, pledging "to work so that all persons on earth may have the opportunity to hear the Gospel in a language they can understand, near where they live."

Billy Kim   The congresses uplifted evangelism throughout the world. Each of us who attended Lausanne, Berlin, or Amsterdam went back to our nations and tried to do greater work because we had attended meetings that had so enhanced evangelism.

"From the stadium, they will walk the half mile or so to Corona Park. Once there, they will run the gauntlet of signs ranging from interpreters' placards offering a multitude of language translation services to virulently anti-Graham messages ('Graham Leads to Hell 800-How-True'; more chillingly, 'God Caused 9/11 800-How-True')."—AUTHORS' NARRATIVE

Opening night of Billy Graham's last Crusade, June 24, 2005, Corona Park, Queens, New York, as people arriving at the site are greeted by volunteer translators holding signs reflecting the city's multiethnic character and by dissenters, some having traveled from as far away as California.—PHOTOGRAPHS BY DEBORAH HART STROBER

"I have kept the ticket from that evening [in 1957, at Madison Square Garden] all these years because it was the day of my salvation."—Lois K. Akehurst

Lois K. Akehurst, who attended Graham's landmark Madison Square Garden Crusade in 1957, comes full circle at Corona Park on June 24, 2005.—PHOTOGRAPH BY DEBORAH HART STROBER

"Billy was an effective preacher. He emulated Bob Jones Sr. with his hand maneuvers, and he had a rapid-paced delivery that was specific to him because of the time he had spent at Bob Jones College."—REV. CHARLES MASSEY

Billy Graham executes a "hand maneuver" as he preaches early in his career.—PHOTOGRAPH BY RUSS BUSBY, COURTESY OF THE BILLY GRAHAM EVANGELISTIC ASSOCIATION

"When the person who was directing the Madison Square Garden Crusade had to leave his post, Billy wanted someone else to take over. But Roger Hull, the lay chairman of the Crusade's executive committee insisted, 'Charlie's our man.'"
—CHARLES RIGGS

Charles Riggs, *left*, and Grady Wilson share a moment during the Jackson, Mississippi, Crusade in 1975.—PHOTOGRAPH BY GERALD S. STROBER

"He saw that I was disappointed and he came to the side of the platform, and he put an arm around my shoulder and said, 'I believe that God has given you a concern to minister to people, and if you stay humble, God will bless and use you.' I remember that arm around my shoulder and the words of encouragement. He didn't reflect on his own disappointment; he was thinking about me."—REV. DR. LEIGHTON FORD, RECALLING GRAHAM'S VISIT TO HIS HIGH SCHOOL IN JANUARY 1949 TO SPEAK AT A YOUTH RALLY.

The Reverend Dr. Leighton Ford, Graham's brother-in-law.
—PHOTOGRAPH COURTESY OF
REV. DR. LEIGHTON FORD

"Ruth deserves a lot of credit for how she so often went through this all alone in raising the children. But I understand that Billy was home more often than people might think; he did his best at being there as often as he could."—ANNA-LISA MADEIRA

"Right now, Billy can hardly hear anything and Ruth can only talk very weakly, so it is very difficult for them to communicate, and so they look at each other and hold hands, which is very poignant right now."—REV. DR. LEIGHTON FORD

Billy and Ruth Graham relax during the 1970s at their home in Montreat. —PHOTOGRAPH BY RUSS BUSBY, COURTESY OF THE BILLY GRAHAM EVANGELISTIC ASSOCIATION

"He was not there to pressure the North Korean government but to encourage it and to offer his personal friendship to their leadership, and his good wishes to their people and his blessings on their society."—STEPHEN LINTON

Billy Graham and Rev. Henry Holley flank President Kim Il Sung of the Democratic People's Republic of Korea [North Korea], *front row, center*, as they stand before a mural during Graham's visit there in the spring of 1992. Others in the front row include Stephen Linton, *far left*; the Reverend Ned Graham; Henry Holley, *fourth from right*; and Dr. Dwight Linton, *far right*.—PHOTOGRAPH BY RUSS BUSBY, COURTESY OF DR. DWIGHT LINTON

Billy and Franklin Graham share a happy moment in 1998 during a Crusade in Ottawa, Canada.—PHOTOGRAPH COURTESY OF THE BILLY GRAHAM EVANGELISTIC ASSOCIATION

"In Cincinnati, just prior to the beginning of his [Graham's] Crusade there in June 2002, he met with Jewish leaders and once again apologized for having spoken negatively to Nixon about Jews so many years earlier."—AUTHORS' NARRATIVE

Some of the 201,600 people Graham preached to at Cincinnati's Paul Brown Stadium during his Crusade there meet with volunteer counselors immediately following their response to the evangelist's invitation.—PHOTOGRAPH BY DEBORAH HART STROBER

"He is a man who has been listed among the ten greatest celebrities of the past twenty years or more, and yet he has remained essentially the same country preacher that he started out being in North Carolina. . . . Fame has never turned his head."—SIDNEY RITTENBERG

"He has a balance in his life that didn't follow the road of being elite and above the average person. He always seemed to keep his humility. He always remembered how he grew up and who he was despite the fame that he achieved." —BEN ARMSTRONG

Graham today, just as he *is.*—PHOTOGRAPH COURTESY OF THE BILLY GRAHAM EVANGELISTIC ASSOCIATION

"Remember, Billy Graham didn't start out to be Billy Graham. God the Holy Spirit took that faithfulness of his and kept expanding it. . . . Nobody's going to be the next Billy Graham. There's only *one.* Franklin is his own man, and . . . he preaches *his* way—and that's very wise."—ROGER PALMS

"It would be a thrill if he [Billy Graham] could come to one of Franklin's festivals. It would also be good for Billy; he is energized when he is with people. I know that Franklin wants him to come anywhere he feels like he can come. . . . Let's pray that will happen."—HENRY HOLLEY

Franklin Graham, just as *he* is in 2006, president of Samaritan's Purse and president and vice chairman of the BGEA.
—PHOTOGRAPH COURTESY OF SAMARITAN'S PURSE

Chapter Five

FROM HARRY S. TRUMAN TO GEORGE W. BUSH

Beginning with Graham's meeting with President Harry S. Truman at the White House in 1950, the evangelist has conferred, and in most instances formed a relationship, with every president whose tenure in office coincided with his active crusade ministry.

Despite the fact that his dealings with the various presidents got off to a rocky start with Truman (Graham and his companions were indiscreet in their comments to the media after their reception in the Oval Office) and although he was never close to John F. Kennedy, he did enjoy close friendships with Dwight D. Eisenhower, Lyndon B. Johnson, Richard M. Nixon, Gerald R. Ford, Jimmy Carter, Ronald Reagan, Bill Clinton, and the Bushes, father and son. They all sought and valued Graham's advice, used him as a sounding board on public opinion, prized his companionship, and asked for his spiritual counsel. In doing so, the chief executives were hardly hesitant in letting it be known both to the media and to the American people that Billy Graham was their friend.

It is not difficult to comprehend the presidents' motives in having granted Graham entry into the Oval Office, their White House family quarters, and their vacation homes, but it is difficult to understand what it was that he received in return. Because he did not require presidential endorsement for his ministry—the huge crowds attending his crusades in the United States and abroad did not do so because of his having visited the Oval Office—Graham's critics, and even some of his supporters, have questioned why, dating from the Johnson era to the recent past, he spent so much time conferring with the various chief executives, his encounters and interactions with them consuming nearly one seventh of the pages of his autobiography.

The obvious explanation for Graham's preoccupation with the ultimate corridor of power could relate to his youth as a farm boy. Could Billy Frank ever have imagined then that he would one day become a much sought-after and revered guest in the White House? A more psychologically based reason for Graham's fascination in being associated with the various presidents could be that he is infatuated with power. The most likely motivation, however, notwithstanding his apparent penchant for name dropping, is that he simply relished the power of *access*—of being able to call presidents on their private telephone lines, have them read and personally respond to his letters, and urge them to take certain actions in crises.

It was understood that Graham enjoyed unusual presidential access; he was constantly implored to raise with the various chief executives all manner of causes and favors that only a president can grant. Thus Billy Graham, though gracious—at times to a fault—was required to discern which issues to promote as well as to exercise great discretion and tact in raising those issues. His access could not be taken for granted—not even with Johnson, with whom Graham was particularly close.

Ben Armstrong   Billy was open to presidents, but they also needed *him*. It was a marriage made in heaven, where he was a part of their lives and they increasingly wanted Billy to give them ideas. They were cognizant of the fact that he had great influence on millions of people.

Gerald Beavan   The presidents had more to gain from association with Billy than he had to gain from them. They felt he was a great icon for them to be affiliated with. I think his purpose in being close to them was to try to impart some spiritual guidance.

Dwight Chapin, campaign worker and appointments secretary to President Nixon   The presidents considered Billy in his spiritual role—as a spiritual being that gave them strength. Billy would pray for the president—that he would have strength—and that engendered openness between him and the various presidents. He was in the lead position; he was working for the big guy in the sky. Therefore, the presidents respected where Billy was coming from. As far as Nixon was concerned, the same thing was true of Norman Vincent Peale.

Ben Armstrong   Many of the evangelicals that are getting involved in the political atmosphere have not themselves achieved the success of Billy Graham. Billy made it—he is not trying to get to the White House; he is *invited* to the White House—and the others are still trying. They tend to think that maybe a political route is what it takes to get known in the changing situation of the world. He had no problem in reaching to the highest levels of society.

Truman

At noon on July 14, 1950, Billy Graham and three of his close associates— Cliff Barrows, Gerald Beavan, and Grady Wilson—were ushered into the Oval Office, where they were greeted by President Truman. The president was not really interested in meeting Graham and his small entourage; he had only agreed to do so following the intervention of John McCormack, a fellow Democrat and an influential member of the House of Representatives from Massachusetts. Although the invitation was extended to Graham alone, he asked, and was granted, permission to bring his associates. Because of the president's initial reluctance to receive Graham, however, McCormack cleared the meeting only on the thirteenth. Graham, then in Winona Lake, Indiana, quickly arranged to travel to Washington by plane.

The meeting was scheduled to last for twenty minutes, its time frame reflecting the lack of importance the president's staff assigned to the young evangelist. Graham began their discussion by describing his recent successes in Los Angeles and Boston (in the latter city, on April 23 he preached to an estimated fifty thousand people gathered on the Boston Common). Graham then attempted to bring the conversation around to the president's spiritual life—an issue that Truman, a Baptist who had married an Episcopalian, was usually loath to discuss. The president cut the conversation short by asserting that he tried "to live by the Sermon on the Mount and the Golden Rule."

Their conversation was taking place less than one month after the outbreak of military hostilities on the Korean peninsula; Graham urged the president to call for a national day of prayer. Listening politely to his suggestion, Truman commented on the conflict. Then, rising, he indicated that the meeting was over.

––––––––––

Gerald Beavan   He was the first president any one of the four of us had ever met, and it was quite impressive to go into the Oval office for the first time. We talked about various things, and to my knowledge the first time that

I ever heard the phrase "police action" was when we were talking about the Korean conflict. He said, "Oh, that's just a police action." When we got through, Billy asked the president, who was a Baptist, if we could have a word of prayer. Truman agreed and Billy prayed for God to bless the president and to bless the United States and help us through the difficulties in Korea.

What occurred next would result in Graham's being banned from the White House for the remaining years of Truman's presidency.

Gerald Beavan   When we came outside, the media was gathered. They asked what the meeting was like and if we had had prayer. Billy told the reporters that we had prayed for God to bless the president. One of them asked if we had knelt in prayer. As a matter of fact, instead of just bowing our heads, we *had,* so they asked us to show them. The four of us all knelt, and that famous photograph was taken.

That visit to the White House having been his first, Graham did not realize the need for adherence to strict protocol—namely, that what transpires in the Oval Office remains confidential; hence his eagerness to provide the media with his relatively detailed account of the meeting.

Gerald Beavan   Truman immediately declared Billy *persona non grata* and wouldn't forgive him for many years. But toward the end of his life he did agree to meet with Billy.

Eisenhower

Vice President Nixon's appearance with Graham on the platform at Yankee Stadium on the afternoon of July 21, 1957, to bring greetings from President Dwight D. Eisenhower marked the first-ever participation by a politician of such high rank in a crusade.

Graham first met Eisenhower in 1952 in France, prior to the famed general's election as president, while he was still serving as commander at the Supreme Headquarters of the Allied Powers in Europe. In the years between their initial meeting and Eisenhower's death in 1969, the two would develop a father-son relationship, one marked by the president's growing interest in religious affiliation. Although Ike's parents were committed Mennonites, he never demonstrated a strong interest in spiritual matters. As president-elect, however, he would ask Billy to recommend a Washington church that he and Mamie could join. On learning that she was a Presbyterian, Graham suggested that the First Couple affiliate with the National Presbyterian Church, whose pastor had served in the military chaplaincy.

The president-elect also sought Graham's advice on a suitable Bible quotation to include in his inaugural address. Graham suggested 2 Chronicles 7:14 ("If my people, which are called by my name, will humble themselves, and pray, and seek my face, and turn from their wicked ways; then I will hear from heaven, and will forgive their sin, and will heal their land").

Graham wrote frequently to the president during the first term, and when Ike contemplated running again in 1956 Graham pledged "my wholehearted support." The two remained friends following Eisenhower's retirement in January 1961 to his farm in Gettysburg, Pennsylvania, in the wake of the election of John Kennedy. Eight years later, several months before Eisenhower's death, Graham visited the critically ill former president in the hospital; Eisenhower sought assurance—as he had in the past—that his sins were forgiven and that he would go to heaven.

Gerald Beavan I had a little one-upmanship on Billy with Eisenhower. H. L. Hunt and Sid Richardson wanted Billy to carry the invitation to Ike to contend for the Republican nomination, so I went over to Europe to Eisenhower's headquarters to try to set up the protocol for Billy's visit the next week. When I finished, the colonel who was showing me around asked if there was anything else I wanted to see, or anyone I wanted to meet. I said, "Yes, I'd like to meet General Eisenhower." So this was arranged and the first time I ever saw Ike he was sitting on the edge of his desk. The first words he said were, "By golly, it's good to see you." When we went back, we went in and Billy and Ike shook hands and Billy turned to me and said, "This is Jerry Beavan." And Ike said, "Oh, Jerry and I are old friends."

Graham's Friendship with Nixon, Kennedy's Election in 1960, and the Forging of a Relationship with the New President

Graham's relationship with President Eisenhower led to the deepening of his friendship with Vice President Nixon, whom he first met in 1950 when Nixon was still a senator from California and the two played a round of golf at the Burning Tree Country Club.

Billy had actually met Nixon's mother, Hannah, a deeply religious Quaker with evangelical leanings, some years before. Then, when Nixon was running for president in 1960 against Senator Kennedy, Graham, though not formally endorsing the former vice president, let it be known that he favored him. To Graham's credit, he did so without engaging in the anti-Catholic vitriol characteristic of a good deal of Protestant opposition to Kennedy.

Some weeks following his victory, Kennedy invited Graham to his father's estate in Palm Beach, Florida. There they played golf, discussed such diverse subjects as the developing situation in Vietnam and the Second Coming of Christ, and appeared together at a news conference during which Graham asserted that the president-elect should be judged not by his religious affiliation but by his "ability and his character."

Though not by any means close to Kennedy, Graham did visit the Oval Office several times during the young leader's thousand days in office. Then, in the fall of 1963, during a visit to Texas to fulfill a preaching obligation in Houston, Graham met with Governor John Connally, who informed him that the president planned to come to that state in November. Several weeks later, during the second week of November, Billy sensed a burden concerning the president's impending visit there and told T. W. Wilson of "an inner foreboding that something terrible was going to happen." At that time, Graham considered contacting Senator George Smathers, of Florida, one of the president's closest friends, to tell him of his burden but then wondered whether it should be brought to Kennedy's attention. On November 22, 1963, Billy was on a golf course in Black Mountain, near his home in Montreat, when he learned that the president had been assassinated.

Johnson

Billy Graham and Lyndon Johnson were particularly close, thanks perhaps to their southern backgrounds. They also had other things in common: both were larger-than-life personalities, excellent speakers, and masters of persuasion, although Graham was not prone to twisting arms in order to achieve his goals. Owing to their rapport, Graham became a frequent guest at both the White House residence and LBJ's ranch in Texas. There they enjoyed each other's company, relaxing by swimming and swapping stories.

They also turned to spiritual matters, reading the Bible and praying together—respites from Johnson's daily concerns about the military conflict then raging in Vietnam. The president wanted his legacy to be his Great Society programs, but he was destined to be preoccupied during his entire presidency with that war, whose escalation was in part due to his own policy. In fact, he was so totally engaged that he personally selected targets for attack by B-52 bombers.

Graham too became engaged in the war effort, albeit in a pastoral manner. Johnson sought his advice on ending the war and Graham traveled to Vietnam in 1966 and 1968, preaching to the troops while avoiding media inquiries as to whether he supported Johnson's policy.

Whether from the stress of the war or, more likely, his deteriorating health, Johnson, who suffered a major heart attack in 1955 and (as Bobby Baker, his chief senatorial aide, stated during an interview for the authors' oral history of the Nixon presidency) had cancerous polyps removed from his throat during his presidency, decided not to seek a second term as president and announced his decision on March 31, 1968. The decision enhanced Nixon's candidacy in 1968.

Nixon

Graham had stood by Nixon following both the former vice president's defeat by Kennedy in 1960 and his ignominious loss to Edmund "Pat" Brown, Sr., in the 1962 gubernatorial race in California. On November 11, just days after the election, Graham, obviously concerned over Nixon's emotional health, wrote to him, "I have thousand of friends but very few close intimate friends. There are few men I have loved as I love you. . . . It would be the greatest tragedy I could think of for you to turn to drink or any of these other escapisms. Millions of Americans admire you as no other man of our time. You have tremendous responsibility to live up to the confidence they have placed in you."

Then, as Nixon began his arduous quest for political rehabilitation in the wake of his electoral debacle in California, Graham encouraged him to seek the presidency yet again.

———————

Dwight Chapin   Billy's visit with Nixon in Key Biscayne [Florida] in December [1967] was a confirmation of Nixon's decision to run; the actual decision had been made some months earlier.

———————

On New Year's Day 1968, Nixon went to see Graham in his room at the Key Biscayne Hotel to ask him one last time whether he should run again; Graham, who was packing to return home, responded, "Dick, I think it is your destiny to be president."

———————

Graham and Nixon During the 1968 Presidential Campaign

Dwight Chapin   In 1968, Billy Graham was holding a crusade in Portland, Oregon, which coincided with the Oregon presidential primary, and Mr. Nixon had a meeting with him in his hotel suite. It was not inconsequential in that we were in the middle of a political campaign. Bobby Kennedy, who was a candidate for the Democratic nomination, was in town at the same time we were. We did not go to the Crusade, although later on Mr. Nixon did go to some crusades. I know that Mr. Graham considered himself neutral but yet I really feel that in 1968 there was no question that he favored Nixon.

I don't remember a religious, fundamentalist component to the "southern strategy." I think there was a feeling that Billy was a distinct advantage, but it came from the basis of their friendship and not from, How do we go out and cultivate this religious group? The friendship was already in place, but there is no question that Billy was a distinct advantage. Billy led Nixon to believe that he favored him in 1968 and that he would do whatever he could do. But he had to be careful in what he did because he was a religious leader and not a political leader. Therefore he would only do things like invite Nixon to a crusade. When Billy invited Nixon to the Knoxville [Tennessee] Crusade [in 1970], Nixon decided that it was probably a very good thing to do. Nobody else would be empowered to say to Nixon, You are going to do this. A decision of that magnitude was *his*; it may have been his idea, along with Billy's. His going to Knoxville was different from going to a rally in Roanoke; his flying in to go to a crusade was a major event. I can remember being back in the holding room, and the stadium was jammed.

During the summer of 1968, following Nixon's second nomination to head the Republican Party's presidential ticket, Graham was on hand in his hotel suite as a group of politicians assisted him in choosing his running mate. Although Graham was reluctant to participate in the discussion, when asked his opinion he recommended Mark Hatfield, a senator from Oregon and a committed evangelical. It was only after returning to his own hotel that Graham learned Nixon had selected as his running mate the little-known governor of Maryland, Spiro Agnew.

Dwight Chapin   Nixon had a number of old friends come into the meeting. It was late in the evening. Billy had been in Miami to offer a prayer earlier that evening at the convention, so Nixon would have known Billy was in Miami and would have been interested in what Billy thought. Senator Hatfield was an old friend of Billy Graham. I've never thought Hatfield was a real possibility. He was not that strong a political type and Oregon was not that important of a state, so from a political point of view Maryland, with Agnew, made more sense.

Though Graham was careful not to explicitly endorse Nixon, in a statement he issued on October 16 responding to attacks on the Republican candidate's integrity he left little doubt of his support for Nixon, observing that his "fellow citizens were looking for a change in the moral and spiritual direction of the nation and that candidates for president should be aware of that fact."

Then, just days after Nixon's election, Graham stated in an interview with the CBS radio program "World of Religion" that "he [Nixon] has a great sense of moral integrity. I think he will be a respected president because I think that will come across to the American people. But I have never seen any indication of, or agreed with, the label that his enemies have given him of 'Tricky Dick.' In the years I've known him, he's never given any indication of being tricky."

Graham's Access to the President

Dwight Chapin   He or T. W. Wilson would call Rose [Rose Mary Woods, Nixon's personal secretary]; she handled all of the old friends. For example, Rose handled Bebe [Rebozo, a very close friend of Nixon's] and she handled Billy. Friends of the president would inform him of an impending overseas trip. Often he would give these people a letter to carry to a foreign leader.

Honor America Day

When the president instituted Sunday morning White House religious services, Graham was frequently either the preacher or the adviser to the president's staff regarding the choice of speaker. The most visible outworking of the Nixon-Graham relationship occurred on July 4, 1970, as Billy joined comedian Bob Hope and Hobart Lewis, the publisher of *Reader's Digest,* in sponsoring Honor America Day, a religious and patriotic rally held at the Lincoln Memorial.

Dwight Chapin   Honor America Day was a huge thing. You have to remember what the Nixon people were going through at the time with the [anti-Vietnam War] demonstrations, and with Honor America Day you had this contrast. We were in San Clemente [Nixon's California home] that day, but we had many of our advance people helping out at the event. We had already planned to be out west; there was no way the president was going to be in Washington. The idea was that the event would be independent of the White House, but we knew every damn thing that happened, as you would imagine.

Gerald Strober   I flew down to Washington the night before with my colleague, Rabbi Marc Tanenbaum. On entering our hotel, we were greeted by George Wilson, who handed us our room keys. The next morning, at the beginning of a typically hot and humid early summer day in the nation's capital, we drove over to the Lincoln Memorial, where I sat in the front section with some of the Graham team members and listened to Archbishop Fulton J. Sheen, astronaut Frank Borman, and finally Billy, the main speaker. For me, the highlight of the day was hearing Kate Smith sing—as only *she* could—Irving Berlin's "God Bless America." There was a discordant note, however: along with the thousands of other attendees, I heard the chants of the anti-Vietnam war protestors gathered behind the rows of seats. When the service ended, as Rabbi Tanenbaum and I were in a limousine en route to the airport with Mr. Borman and Archbishop Sheen, the car had slowed in exiting from the Memorial area and a young man in the crowd indicated that the archbishop should roll down his window. Assuming, perhaps, that he was about to be asked to offer a blessing, the archbishop was instead startled—as were the rest of us—when the youth shouted an unprintable epithet suggesting that the prelate had engaged in unnatural sexual activity.

The Nature of the President's Personal Relationship with Graham

Dwight Chapin   It was a "guy thing." Mrs. Nixon definitely knew Billy. The whole Nixon family was fond of Billy; everybody liked Billy. What was there *not* to like about this guy? [The president's chief of staff, H. R.] Haldeman had a very, very good relationship with him. In their meetings away from

Washington, the men would act like two good friends. The atmosphere was very congenial, and the Nixon stiffness and awkwardness that we are all familiar with didn't seem to be that way around Billy. Nixon was always very good, one on one; they would laugh and have a good time together.

In dealing with Israel, Graham was never loath to seek assistance from American presidents, as he did with President Nixon at a particularly crucial moment in the Jewish state's battle for survival.

Gerald Strober   On April 30, 1972, I was in Atlanta when I received an urgent call from Rabbi Tanenbaum in New York. He informed me that the Nixon administration was holding up a shipment of F-15 fighter planes. The rabbi then asked me to go to see Billy and to seek his help. I called T. [T. W. Wilson] in Montreat and he told me that Billy, following a conversation early that morning with President Nixon, was already on his way to the White House.

Earlier, during a telephone conversation, President Nixon had told Billy that he would make a nationwide televised address from the Oval Office that evening announcing that U.S. forces had bombed Cambodia and wanted the evangelist to be close at hand as he spoke to the nation. Sensing the urgency of the situation, however, T. said, "Give me the particulars of the Israeli situation and I will relate them to Billy." Later that afternoon, T. called me. He said that he had talked to Billy, who wanted to assure us that he would raise the F-15 issue with the president.

On a Thursday evening early in December of 1973, just weeks after Israel, under the leadership of Prime Minister Golda Meir, had defeated Egypt and Syria in the very bitterly fought and costly Yom Kippur War, T. called me at home late one evening. He said that Billy, who considered Mrs. Meir a close friend, wanted to invite her—she was then visiting Washington—to attend the Crusade he was holding at the Kiel Auditorium, in St. Louis, Missouri. While cognizant of the political implications of such an invitation, Billy wanted Mrs. Meir to address the thousands of people who would attend the Saturday evening session. Billy also realized that his powerful message of support for Israel, a nation still reeling from the effects of war, was bound to be front-page news and that that Sunday morning's newspapers throughout the United States would likely carry a photograph of him greeting Mrs. Meir.

I told T. that I would call him back as soon as possible. I then telephoned Rabbi Tanenbaum, who in turn placed a call to Simcha Dinitz, Israel's ambassador to the United States, who at that very moment was hosting Mrs. Meir and Secretary of State Henry Kissinger at a late dinner at his official residence in Washington, D.C. The ambassador, after being told of Billy's offer, promised to raise the question with the Israeli prime minister immediately. About an hour after I received T.'s call, Rabbi Tanenbaum called me again, this time to say that while Mrs. Meir was extremely grateful for the invitation—I was to communicate these specific words to T.—she had to return to Israel after the Sabbath ended on Saturday evening in order to be able to preside at the scheduled Sunday meeting of her cabinet.

Billy then called me, saying that he really needed to talk to the prime minister, so much so that he was going to have a direct, private telephone line installed in his hotel room for that purpose. He asked me to travel to Washington the next day and call him. He would, by then, have the private number, which I would then give to Mrs. Meir. Later that Friday, the two friends had a long—and as Billy later described to me, very productive—conversation.

He also told me that during the war he had three conversations with President Nixon. We do not know now—perhaps future historians will—what influence the evangelist had on the president. What we do know is that at a very critical juncture, the United States launched a massive airlift of materiel to Israel and that at the moment the Soviet leadership threatened to intervene on the Arab side the president ordered a worldwide alert of U.S. forces.

Following the president's resignation, Billy visited Nixon at his home in California. And when Nixon moved back to the East Coast, the two would meet in New York.

Lane Adams   I asked Billy what he thought of Nixon's resignation and this business of the tapes. He answered that President Nixon surrounded himself with people, none of whom believed in sin. He said that for eighteen months before the resignation, Nixon's staff had made it impossible for him to get through to the president. And he added that he learned later that they made it almost impossible for the president to get out and find Billy, although he was available. He thanked God for that because it meant that he was distanced from Nixon during the last part of the presidency. But he continued to be his friend and would go out and visit with him in San Clemente. If Billy had one fault, it was that when he loved you and you were his friend he exaggerated your virtues. One time he introduced me and I thought he was introducing somebody else.

Graham also preached at both Pat and Richard Nixon's funerals. At the former president's rite, which took place on April 27, 1994, at the Nixon Library, in Yorba Linda, California, Graham observed: "I think most of us have been staggered by the many things that he accomplished during his life. . . . He had great respect for the Office of the President. I never heard him one time criticize a living president who was in the office at that time. There's an old Indian saying: 'Never criticize a man until you've walked a mile in his shoes.'"

Graham maintains his connection to the Nixon family in his friendships with the Nixons' daughters, Julie Eisenhower and Tricia Cox.

Graham's Relationships with Other Presidents

Ford

Billy Graham knew and respected Gerald Ford from the Michigan politician's twenty-five years as a member of the House of Representatives. When Ford succeeded to the presidency in August 1974, Graham graciously offered counsel to the new president's close friend and longstanding spiritual adviser, the Reverend Billy Zeoli, a Christian film executive from Grand Rapids.

Graham became involved in Ford's highly controversial pardon of Richard Nixon, an action that likely resulted in Ford's loss to Jimmy Carter in 1976. Citing concern over both Nixon's health (the former president had developed a serious blood disorder) and the deleterious effect of the Watergate scandal on the nation, as well as Nixon's role in it, Graham contacted several Republican political leaders close to Nixon and Ford and recommended a pardon. It is difficult to discern exactly what influence Graham's view had on Ford, who called him only a few days before issuing the pardon, but surely his endorsement provided Ford with significant political cover.

Dwight Chapin   I can envision Billy just moving off and seeking a pardon and I can also envision Nixon, through an intermediary, asking Billy to do that.

Carter

Jimmy Carter served as honorary chairman of two of Graham's Atlanta Crusades in 1973, while governor of Georgia and again in 1994, following his sole term as president.

Graham and Carter had at least four things in common: they were products of the semirural south, identified as born-again Christians, were members of Southern Baptist churches, and were Democrats (Graham in terms of his voter registration rather than allegiance to the party). The Grahams were also occasionally overnight guests at the White House. But the two men were not especially close during Carter's presidency.

Although Graham sympathized with Carter—as had many others—in 1978, when the president was confronted by and had to deal with the crisis precipitated when Islamic extremists seized the U.S. embassy in Tehran, Iran, the evangelist appeared to have considered Carter a well-intentioned but inept leader.

Reagan

Michael Deaver   He [Reagan] was deeply religious; from the standpoint of living the Christian religion, he was probably the greatest Christian I had known. And he treated everyone the same: forgave and never held anger or was disagreeable with people. He deeply believed in the simplicity of the Christian faith and the Gospels.

In Sacramento [in the late 1960s], I went into to Governor Reagan's office, and he was sitting there drinking from a bottle of an antacid. I asked him what he was doing and he replied that his stomach was bothering him. Several weeks later, I went in and said, "I haven't seen you drinking out of that antacid bottle." He said, "Mike, I kept looking over my shoulder for the answers and realized if I looked *straight up* I could get them. I haven't needed that bottle ever since."

Reagan's Relationship with Graham

Michael Deaver   I assume that there was political compatibility, but it was based more on a spiritual rather than a political connection. Reagan was extremely spiritual, a literal Christian; he believed he had been reborn in Christ. He would have looked forward to meeting Billy Graham and learning from him rather than the other way around. Ronald Reagan wanted a private conversation to reaffirm issues of his faith or simply to have the comfort of Dr. Graham in his presence. It would simply be unlike Reagan to say, "Oh gosh, we're in a jam; let's get Billy down here and get a photo op." That would never have happened.

William Martin In 1979 and 1980, when many fundamentalists and evangelicals were getting involved in politics with the rise of the religious right, he [Graham] was warning against it. He said it was easy for preachers lacking proper information to be manipulated and used, sometimes cynically, so he recognized that it was safer to withdraw. While he continued to have friendships with Reagan, and particularly with the Bushes, he has not tried to be involved in the actual political aspects.

The 1980 Presidential Campaign

Michael Deaver The reason Reagan ran in 1980 was because he thought it was his destiny—which was based on his religious faith—to get the Soviets to the table and end the cold war.

Why Didn't Reagan Seek Graham's Help in the Crucial North Carolina Primary?

Michael Deaver It might have been something that occurred to the political people, but it wasn't something Reagan would have ever used. Reagan would never use anybody, and certainly he would never mix up or jeopardize the spiritual relationship that he so much wanted and needed with Billy Graham for politics.

The so-called Reagan Revolution began on November 4, 1980, when the former film star and governor of California thwarted Jimmy Carter's quest for a second term. Reagan's victory was made possible in large part by the advocacy and voter registration drive implemented by the Moral Majority, an organization founded in June 1979 by the Reverend Jerry Falwell, then the little-known pastor of Thomas Road Baptist Church in Lynchburg, Virginia.

The Moral Majority's goal was to unite religious and political conservatives in a common agenda. The organization's platform was prolife, protraditional family, promoral, and pro-American, including advocacy of both a strong national defense and support for the State of Israel. In theory, Graham could subscribe to the Moral Majority's program because his preaching had always reflected regard for the sanctity of life, the centrality of the family in human experience, and the need for adherence to a set of biblically oriented moral principles. He had by the late 1970s become an internationally renowned personality; he remained an American patriot deeply concerned for his nation's future.

At the same time, Graham had been burned by Watergate. As one whose *raison d'être* is the winning of lost souls, he realized in his very public association with Nixon the potential cost to his ministry of identifying too closely with wielders of political power. Thus, rather than affiliate with the promulgators of this new surge of evangelical interest in partisan politics, Graham was determined to focus on bringing the Gospel to areas of the world then under communist domination. So during the Reagan era, while maintaining his longstanding friendship with the president, Graham ceded the political field to the increasingly visible and confrontational Reverend Falwell and his associates.

Michael Deaver   There is no question that the Moral Majority helped elect Ronald Reagan in 1980. They may have tipped the balance in Texas and in the South, but the fundamental Catholic beliefs in Pennsylvania, New Jersey, and Ohio also helped. Reagan was very funny about all of that. We were running against a guy [Jimmy Carter] who wore his religion on his sleeve. That was offensive to Reagan; it was something he wouldn't do. We were in Dallas at a Christian broadcasters' event, and we were just mobbed coming out. This young woman grabbed him by the lapel and asked, "Do you believe?" And Reagan stopped and answered, "Yes, of course." And she said, "No, no, are you *reborn?*" I never heard him be asked or answer that question again, but he looked at her deadly seriously and said, "Yes." To him, that was a private conversation despite the fact that we were followed by thirty or so reporters in this wedge of people trying to leave the auditorium.

Reagan's Religious Practice as President

Michael Deaver   The president stopped going to church because he thought it was such an imposition for the parishioners to go through security devices, so they had little services at Camp David. And sometimes at the residence Dr. Graham or others would come in and they would have prayers.

Graham's Closeness to the First Family

Michael Deaver   There was always social interaction between Billy and both Ronald and Nancy Reagan. There were luncheons, dinners, or coffee; usually when he came to Sacramento, Los Angeles, or Washington, it was a social visit. Dr. Graham would let the Reagans know he was going to be in town and a meeting would be arranged. Their meetings were almost exclusively private. The Reagans did not want to make a big deal out of Billy Graham coming to the White House. Many times his visits were not even on the schedule.

Graham was personally close to the Reagans (he was a more frequent overnight guest at the White House during the Reagan era than in the Johnson and Nixon years), but there were political aspects to their relationship in that the president endorsed Graham's controversial trip to the Soviet Union in 1984.

Michael Deaver   Reagan would have been interested in Dr. Graham's visits to the Soviet Union. He was soaking up information on the subject and he was learning about the Soviet people and the fact that they were still practicing religion. He got evangelicals and Jewish refuseniks out of the Soviet Union. Teddy [Senator Edward M.] Kennedy had advised him to do this privately rather than making a big deal out of it publicly. Reagan took that advice and tried it and it worked and he got a number of people out by simply giving the names. I know that in his meetings with high-ranking Soviet officials he would give them a piece of paper with some names on it and never say anything more about it. But people got out.

When Reagan came back from his first meeting with [Mikhail] Gorbachev—I had already left the White House—he asked me over to tell me all about it, and at the end of the conversation Reagan said to me, "I think he [Gorbachev] believes." I said, "Are you telling me that the chairman of the Soviet Union believes in God?" And Reagan responded,

"He believes in a higher power; I know that." That was really the basis for Reagan to connect there. I would not be surprised if he had discussed this with Dr. Graham [before Graham went to the Soviet Union].

Graham supported Reagan's innovative idea of sending a resident ambassador to the Vatican. In an even more contentious action, in 1981 Graham lobbied various senators on behalf of the president's sale of AWAC aircraft to Saudi Arabia, a foreign policy decision strenuously opposed by the Moral Majority.

Gerald Strober   I first met Jerry Falwell in 1978, when I coordinated a visit to Israel by a group of leading evangelicals. As a result of that trip, Reverend Falwell and Prime Minister Menachem Begin became close friends and Falwell became Israel's most visible, vocal, and powerful ally within the evangelical community. While I was well aware that the Moral Majority was against the AWAC sale, I did not know that Billy Graham, who was always a staunch friend of the Jewish state, had supported the administration on the issue. I only learned that when Falwell telephoned me late one evening to say that an aide of Reagan's who had attempted to influence him to change his mind had used the argument that *Billy Graham* supported the president's position.

Graham Comforts the Reagans

Michael Deaver   Billy Graham and Mrs. Reagan were very close. He gave her great comfort when the president was shot. And he visited the Reagans during the Alzheimer's period; it was clearly more helpful to Nancy than to the president by that time. Billy and I talked about whether he was going to be able to handle the Reagan funeral. He had called and said that for reasons of health he didn't think he could preside. That was when we went for [Senator] John Danforth, who was a good choice because he was an Episcopal priest.

Although Graham did not preside at the president's funeral on June 9, 2004, he issued a statement observing that "Ronald Reagan was one of my closest friends for many years. Ruth and I spent a number of nights at the White House and had hundreds of hours of conversation with the president and the First Lady. Mr. Reagan had a religious faith deeper than most people knew. . . . The President was a man of tremendous integrity, based on his religious belief."

Bush Forty-One

Billy Graham called Jerry Falwell in the summer of 1980, immediately following the Republican National Convention, to ask him whether he was upset over presidential nominee Reagan's selection of Bush as his running mate. Falwell (who would become a good friend of the Bush family) told us when we interviewed him for our oral history of the Reagan presidency that he had replied, "Billy, I'll just pray that God will give Ronald Reagan eight years of wonderful health." [It should be noted that Falwell and Bush have since become close friends.—authors]

Following a pattern that evolved in the wake of the Nixon debacle, Billy had a warm relationship with Bush, as he would with the president's successor, Bill Clinton, spending time—occasionally in Ruth's company—with the First Family at their estate in Kennebunkport, Maine, or in the White House. It was while visiting the Bushes in the Executive Mansion on the evening of January 16, 1991, that Graham, having joined them for dinner, heard momentous news that would have repercussions even to this day. Sitting with Barbara Bush on a couch in the Blue Room, with their attention focused on a television monitor as the president addressed the American people, Billy and the First Lady learned that the first Gulf War had just begun.

Clinton

Bill Clinton first saw Graham in person when, as a teenager, he attended a crusade in Little Rock, Arkansas. The two actually met in 1985, at a session during the National Governors' Conference. Four years later, Clinton served as honorary chairman of Graham's Little Rock Crusade. Then in 1992, when he accepted president-elect Clinton's invitation to offer a prayer at his inauguration, some evangelicals criticized him for identifying with a politician whose views clashed with those of the religious right.

Two years later, in 1994, Graham briefed President Clinton on his long meeting in North Korea with Kim Il Sung, presumably providing the president with insight into that nation's closed society as well as transmitting a personal message from the Paramount Leader.

Then, in the wake of the scandal of the president's involvement with a White House intern, as it became increasingly certain that he would be impeached, although Graham maintained public silence he did pray for the Clinton family. As Clinton said of his relationship with Graham during an interview with Larry King on CNN, "I kept in touch with him over the years and saw him in the White House. He was uncommonly kind to me and Hillary, and always wise in his counsel and firm in his guidance."

Bush Forty-Three

Graham was especially close to the Bush family. During the summer of 1985, George H. W. Bush invited him to spend a weekend at the family's vacation home in Kennebunkport, Maine. On that Sunday, Graham preached at a small local church, and that evening the former president asked him to respond to questions posed by members of the Bush family.

It was during this weekend that the former president's son, George W. Bush, who as a young man had abused alcohol, was challenged as he heard Graham's words to examine his own life and values. As Bush recalled in his book *A Charge to Keep*, "What he said sparked a change in my heart. I don't remember the exact words. It was more the power of his example. The Lord was so clearly reflected in his gentle and loving demeanor." The next morning, as the two men strolled along Walker Beach, George W. Bush was once again impressed by Graham's nonjudgmental approach, recalling that "he didn't lecture or admonish; he shared warmth and concern. Billy Graham didn't make you feel guilty; he made you feel loved. Over the course of that weekend, Reverend Graham planted a mustard seed in my soul, a seed that grew over the next year. He led me to the path and I began walking. It was the beginning of a change in my life."

Chapter Six

BILLY GRAHAM'S VISION
FOR THE WORLD

Millie Dienert   One morning when we were relaxing with the Grahams, Mr. Graham said to me, "Millie, the Lord has told me that you should go to England and encourage God's people to pray." If anybody had hit me in the head with a hammer, it couldn't have been more drastic to me. I just sat there and said, "Well the Lord hasn't told *me*." And he replied, "You didn't *ask* Him."

Out of that conversation evolved my going into fifty-nine countries. The purpose of it all was to do what he concentrated on. If ever there was a man who was dependent on the prayers of God's people, it was him. When he would be asked about the most important preparatory aspects of his ministry, he would always answer, "There are three of them: the first is prayer, the second is prayer, the third is prayer." The intensity of his ministry was always focused on the intensity of prayer support.

Roger Palms   We would have a team gathering at a crusade, so there was always a chance to talk with Billy. He expected his editor to attend the crusade; you can't write about evangelistic meetings if you don't attend them. Every crusade was different; Bombay was not Boston.

Graham's Impact on Colleagues

Billy Kim   My first impression of him when we met in Seoul [in 1973] was of a humble man, an honest, genuine, and caring person.

Bill Brown   I had first met him in Albuquerque; he was very humble and very kind and very encouraging. He was dynamic behind the pulpit, which was quite different [from the way he was] in person.

Roger Palms   Billy is transparent; what you see on the platform is what you get in private conversation. There's not two; there's only *one* Billy Graham; he is what he *is*. He's also a learner. If he were coming to your city for a crusade, he would start taking the local newspapers ahead of time to see what was happening in your community. Then he'd bring the clergy together and ask them about their problems and needs. His mind is sharp, yet he is always trying to learn and grow. That pleased local pastors and people in other nations. He wasn't the kind of American coming in to show people how to do it; he came in as a humble servant of the church. Over the years people came to appreciate that he is an evangelist who is a servant.

Dwight Linton, uncle of Stephen Linton; missionary in Korea for twenty-five years; interpreter to Graham on his first visit to North Korea, 1992   I had met Billy Graham sometime before, but this was the first time I got to know him. There are many things that come together to make up my impression of him. One, of course, is simply his reputation. I was impressed with his ability to communicate with just about anyone. Also, you could just call him an old-fashioned southern gentleman. He is a very kind person, very humble, and that comes across when you're talking with him.

Betty Bao Lord, author, human rights activist; wife of Winston Lord, U.S. ambassador to the People's Republic of China during Billy and Ruth Graham's first visit   He is a very dignified and a very gentle person. I am not a very tall person and I was impressed by his height. It's always impressive when you see him. Many times you meet people in person that you have seen in photographs or on television and they look different. He looked the way he was *supposed* to look.

Stephen Linton, nephew of Dr. Dwight Linton; chairman, Eugene Bell Foundation; consultant and interpreter to Graham on visits to North Korea, 1992 and 1994 Mr. Graham is very gracious; he spent time even learning how to bow like a Korean [prior to his first visit to North Korea]. I don't think he ever visited a country he didn't think was the best country in the world, or the most beautiful. He's very ingratiating in a very positive sense.

Millie Dienert He had rapport with leaders in this world because he was not an attacker; he never attacked a problem or a person. He prayed about any situation he had with those people. Before he was going to meet with a leader, if there was a group of us around he would always say, "Pray for me. At 11:30 I'm going to see so and so. Pray that I will say what God wants me to say." His one desire was to show the person that Jesus really lived in *his* life and that he would like the person to know Jesus too.

Winston Lord, U.S. ambassador to the People's Republic of China during Billy and Ruth Graham's first visit; husband of Betty Bao Lord You fall into trite clichés about this man, but I was not surprised by what I found. I expected a person who radiated goodness and tolerance and dignity, and that's what he is in private. I don't want to compare him to the Dalai Lama—they are both great people—but both men have a gentle, conciliatory approach. You know they have ironclad convictions. It doesn't mean they are weak; just the opposite—sort of a nonviolent approach. Graham announced publicly before he arrived in China, and certainly in any press conference he held while he was there, that his basic style on issues like religious freedom would be to press with some moderation, and *privately,* as opposed to taking on the Chinese head-on. One can agree or disagree with this tactic, but that is clearly his conviction and likely consistent with what he does with all these issues. He is, after all, a man who with total tolerance and sincerity has been a friend of many presidents who have tremendous ideological differences and he crosses the whole spectrum. He is a very religious man but also a very tolerant man, and certainly someone who made a very good impression in China, as well as with us personally.

Betty Bao Lord I think that in general they wouldn't be upset [with his earlier strident anticommunist views] because they know that almost everybody was anticommunist—they had dealt with Nixon, who was the biggest anticommunist before he made the China opening—so they are very pragmatic in their approach to foreigners. If Billy Graham had been Chinese, it would have been different, but they take for granted most foreigners with an anticommunist background. They will just shower him with hospitality; that is their Chinese way of dealing with "barbarians."

Bill Brown   In going to communist countries, I believe he tried to analyze his influence on individuals, not only the impact of what a crowd of people finding the Lord would make but also what other influence he could have on the lives of some of the leaders.

Winston Lord   Not speaking for myself, just being analytical, some people would say that, depending on the audience, an attitude of tolerance doesn't get you very far, that some of these repressive regimes and individuals are happy to be let off the hook. It's fine with them to keep everything at a very polite, general level. That is the vulnerability people with Mr. Graham's and the Dalai Lama's approach face. Some people will say they are not tough enough. But given Mr. Graham's success over his long career of winning converts and admirers, it's pretty hard to second-guess him. I also think he is probably a very realistic person who recognized that he was not going to bring about religious freedom in China overnight—that it's a long-term haul and perhaps he could be more effective with his approach than with a direct, confrontational one.

Sidney Rittenberg, academician, business consultant; prisoner of People's Republic of China for sixteen years; interpreter for Graham on trips to China, 1988, 1992, and 1994   When my wife and I came back from China in 1979, we happened to see one of Billy's crusades on television. We both felt that this is a man that [it] would be very good to get to China because he was so obviously sincere and direct. We didn't make any attempt to contact him. But then I went to China in 1981 with Mike Wallace and the "Sixty Minutes" team. We made three programs and after they were broadcast we received a handwritten note from Billy and Ruth saying that they had enjoyed the programs and hoped that we would continue to tell the American people the truth about China. Then someone who worked for Graham contacted us and raised the possibility of Billy and Ruth going to China.

We worked on that from the beginning of 1982 until 1988, when the Grahams made a very successful trip.

Betty Bao Lord   Sidney became quite popular with visiting delegations because of his many years in China, as well as his grasp of the language. Many people tried to help him because he had suffered so much during the Cultural Revolution. I introduced him to Mike Wallace, and others used him to facilitate their visits because he is an excellent translator.

Traveling the World for Christ

Australia, the Late 1950s

Bill Brown   Jerry [Beavan] was a very clever man. One of the things he would say to me was, "Bill, always try to do something new in each city you go to." In Sydney, where I worked for about a year in 1958 and 1959, we were having trouble raising the Crusade budget. At that time, Joan and I were supporting a Korean orphan by donating three dollars a month to World Vision. I asked Jerry, "Why can't we borrow the World Vision plan?" So we started the prayer partnership that has brought millions of dollars to help fund crusades.

Monaco, Early 1960s

Ben Armstrong   In Monte Carlo, Monaco, thanks to the generosity of Prince Rainier and his beautiful wife, Grace Kelly, we were able to secure a long-time leasing arrangement for Trans World Radio—a company I had organized with my father-in-law—to broadcast "The Hour of Decision" on Radio Monaco. The president of Holiday Inns had given Billy Graham a place to stay and Billy became a regular visitor. In the two years that my wife and I were there, we were able to see him, and he visited a Protestant church in downtown Monaco.

London, 1966

Lane Adams   When I joined the team, Billy asked me to move to London to work with ministers in advance of his Crusade there. I met with him in Omaha, where he was holding a Crusade, and suggested that I was not qualified for this assignment. Billy insisted that I was, and when our discussion ended I felt that he had taken a canvas and placed it on an easel and had taken a paint brush and made a couple of strokes around the fringes. It was as if he was saying, The whole picture will look like *this*; you fill it in. And with that he would hand you the paint brush. What was interesting was his trust that you could do that. When the meeting ended, I remarked to Walter Smyth that the session had not turned out as I had planned, and Walter replied, "That frequently happens when you talk to Billy."

Before leaving for London, I met with Billy in his private office at the team office in Atlanta. He asked that we get down on our knees and pray. I have often wished that I had a tape recording of that prayer. I had never heard a man pour out his heart as he did for the people he loved so dearly. To this day, I am touched at the remembrance of it.

Howard Jones   Billy asked me to go over ahead of time to make contacts in the Brixton neighborhood, where people of color from many different parts of the world lived. I arrived and checked into the hotel where a number of team members were to stay. I signed the register, left my bags with the front desk clerk, and headed off to a meeting. While I was gone, the lady who owned the hotel examined the register and said, "Oh, we have a Reverend Howard O. Jones; he must be a Welshman." The clerk said, "No, he's an African American. He's with the Billy Graham team." The owner, after reminding the clerk that the hotel did not accommodate blacks, called the Billy Graham office and told our staff that I could not stay in the hotel. She added that if I were not back soon, she would have my luggage put out on the street. When I was told of this conversation, I was very upset. But Walter Smyth said that he had already wired Billy, who was en route to England by ocean liner, and that Billy had already wired back with instructions to cancel all the team reservations in the hotel. He told Walter, "If Howard can't stay there, none of them will stay there." The experience left me sick to my stomach. I wanted to take the next plane back to New York. But the Lord began to deal with me; he reminded me of His suffering. I thought: I can't run out on You, nor on Billy.

The Philippines, 1977

Henry Holley   We had held crusades in both Hong Kong and in Taipei in 1975 and a delegation from Manila came to those events and were quite impressed by what they saw. I was the crusade director in Manila in

1977. The Crusade was held at Rizal Park, at Manila Bay. That was a great Crusade; we had 150,000 people on the closing day.

Roger Palms When we were in the Philippines, President [Ferdinand] Marcos gave a dinner for Billy and the team. When my turn came to shake the president's hand, Billy talked about me as if I were a great writer. He told the president what I was doing. I thought, My goodness; it's like they were giving the dinner for *me*. But that was Billy; he'd always push other people, including his staff, and give them recognition. *He* didn't have to be the important man; he made *us* important. He was comfortable with himself. He is without guile—he has no ego to stroke—and that is why people want to do 110 percent for him, because he is not gathering anything for himself. In his early years in the ministry, he remarked that "if God took his hand off me, there's nothing here."

The Soviet Union

Graham, accompanied by Grady Wilson, first visited Moscow in 1959, where he prayed that he might one day preach. In those days—the heart of the cold war—such a prayer was unlikely to be answered soon. Nor were Soviet officials likely to overlook the fact that his preaching reflected a hard-line position concerning his belief that communism was a threat to Christian values.

More than a decade following the visit to Moscow, he met Dr. Alexander Haraszti, a Hungarian-born former pastor and physician, who with his wife had immigrated to the United States in 1956, shortly after the Hungarian revolution. Haraszti settled in Atlanta, where he became acquainted with some of Graham's associates, leading to Graham's being invited to visit and preach in Hungary and Poland.

Then, in 1982, following strenuous efforts by Haraszti to secure an invitation for Graham to preach in the Soviet Union, one was forthcoming from no less a religious personage than Patriarch Pimen, the head of the Russian Orthodox Church, who asked Graham to attend a conference of religious leaders from around the world, scheduled to take place in Moscow in May. The patriarch designated that meeting the World Conference of Religious Workers for Saving the Sacred Gift of Life from Nuclear Catastrophe.

A college freshman would likely have concluded that the conference was aimed at spreading communist propaganda at America's expense, but Graham—after consulting his friends Kissinger, Nixon, and Reagan—decided to attend. By accepting the invitation, Graham would have the opportunity to preach in two churches in Moscow, as well as to meet with Russian Jewish leaders. He would also enter the diplomatic minefield located in the basement of the American Embassy, where six Siberian Pentecostals had taken refuge in 1978.

The news that Graham planned to visit Moscow and participate in Patriarch Pimen's conference caused dismay among many American evangelicals and human rights advocates. In a statement issued on the eve of his departure for Moscow, Graham declared, "It is my sincere prayer that this visit will make at least a small contribution to better understanding between the peoples of the Soviet Union, the United States, and other countries of the world. We trade with each other, we have cultural exchanges, and we have continued political negotiations in spite of our differences. I think it is now time that we move into a spiritual dimension as well. My purpose in going to the Soviet Union is spiritual, and it is not my intention to become involved in political or ideological issues."

Whatever his intention, Graham ended up mired in controversy from almost the moment of his arrival in Moscow. There he was followed by a large media contingent eager to obtain his view of religious freedom in the Soviet Union. Because he did not wish to alienate his hosts, he tried to suggest that it did exist to a degree within that nation. As he stated during a press conference, "It would seem to me that in the [two] churches I have visited in the Soviet Union, and there are thousands of them, services are allowed to go on freely." It is true that approximately one thousand people attended the service in the Moscow Baptist Church (where he preached on the paralytic man depicted in the Gospel of John), but it is also true that two-thirds of the attendees were journalists, conference delegates, or security officers.

During the course of his sermon, Graham quoted from Romans 13:1: "Let every soul be subject unto the higher powers." Though his interpretation was consistent with a literal understanding of the Scriptures, he surely was not suggesting that the Soviet believers should submit to their totalitarian masters. Unfortunately, a wire service account stated, *inaccurately,* that he had used the verse from Romans as his text. Graham later allowed that it might have been better had he omitted that reference.

When he addressed the conference, Graham did express his concern that the Soviet Union was not living up to its obligations as a signatory to the UN Universal Declaration of Human Rights and the Helsinki Final Act. On the other hand, he also expressed what may be charitably described as a naïve sense of daily life in the Soviet Union, having informed a reporter that "the meals I have had are among the finest I have ever eaten. In the United States you have to be a millionaire to have caviar, but I have had caviar with almost every meal."

A further problem concerned his meeting with the Pentecostals, who badgered him with questions related to both their situation and the status of 147 religious workers imprisoned by the Soviet authorities. At the visit's end, it was obvious that Graham—now the subject of attacks from both the religious right and human rights campaigners—had suffered a severe public relations reversal.

In a CBS News commentary, Bill Moyers, a former aide to President Johnson and a friend of Graham's, appeared to sum up the feelings of many Americans when he stated (as quoted in William Martin's *A Prophet with Honor*) that "religious freedom is tolerated so long as you don't exercise it. Billy Graham did not miss this so much as he ignored it, partly from southern courtesy, partly for tactical reasons, partly as the price of celebrity. He's a popular and pleasant fellow who doesn't like offending his hosts, whether in Washington or Moscow. But it's never easy to sup with power and get up from the table spotless. That's why the prophets of old preferred the wilderness. When they came forth, it was not to speak softly with kings and governors, but to call them to judgment."

Graham returned to the Soviet Union in 1984, preaching to thousands of people in a four-city tour. During a meeting with Boris Ponomarev, a high-ranking Soviet official, Graham said that "a major reason the American public does not support closer ties with the Soviet Union is because of what is perceived as religious discrimination and even oppression." Graham also cautioned Ponomarev: "You will never reach a satisfactory understanding with the United States as long as you keep up this anti-Semitic and anti-Christian thing. Many Americans are concerned over the very low number of Jews who have been permitted to migrate from the Soviet Union in the last year or two, and other issues affecting people of Jewish background, such as rabbinical training and language teaching in Hebrew. It is difficult for détente to be successful as long as these problems remain."

Graham and the Plight of Soviet Jewry

Years earlier, Graham had expressed a keen interest in the plight of Jews suffering under the yoke of Soviet oppression.

Gerald Strober   In 1971, a time of particular difficulty for Soviet Jewry, a woman named Rivka Alexandrovich came to the AJC's [American Jewish Committee's] office seeking our help in obtaining the release of her daughter, Ruth, a Jewish human rights activist, from a Moscow prison. Rivka, who had immigrated to Israel, was a strong-willed, courageous person. Soon after meeting her, we took her to Rochester, New York, to address the general assembly of the United Presbyterian Church, where Rivka, the first Jew ever to address the Presbyterians' annual meeting, electrified the audience.

At the same time, we realized that the leaders of a mainline Protestant denomination were not likely to influence the conservative Nixon administration. When we returned to our hotel, I placed a call to T. [T. W. Wilson] in Montreal. He told me that Billy was at that moment having his hair cut in the barbershop of the Madison Hotel, in Washington. I then called the hotel, asked to be connected to the barbershop, and then to Billy. When he came on the line and heard about Rivka's situation, he asked us to bring her in three days' time to Chicago, where he was preparing for a crusade.

On arriving in Chicago, we taxied over to the Conrad Hilton Hotel and were ushered into Billy's suite, where he and Rivka proceeded to have a long conversation. Billy was taking detailed notes and after about forty-five minutes he pulled a small address-type book from his pocket and picked up a telephone and said, "Hello. This Billy Graham. Is Henry there?"

"Henry" was Henry A. Kissinger. Billy soon hung up and said, "Dr. Kissinger is with the president. They are in Key Biscayne and Henry will call me back." Five minutes later the telephone rang. "Hello, Henry," Billy said. And then, referring to his notes, he went on to explain in detail Ruth Alexandrovich's plight. One month later, the young woman joined her mother, Rivka, in Israel.

Dwight Chapin   Henry was very easy to get along with, as long as people weren't into policy. Henry always liked the celebrities that were around, and to Henry Billy was a celebrity. I would think that Henry really got a kick out of knowing Billy. I knew Henry so well, traveled with him on the China breakthrough, and I know how celebrity-type things would get his attention. Maybe Billy looked at it the same way. One day, I flew with Henry by helicopter to Santa Monica, and this gorgeous woman [the actress Jill St. John] picked him up. Those were Henry's debonair days. He was on a roll; he loved the glitz of it all.

Ben Armstrong   Billy was like a magical voice in the Western world. Whatever he did, he had the attention of hundreds of millions of people. This mellowed him to become more understanding of other cultures. He had great success in Eastern Europe, although he had opposition from the right.

William Martin   He had a very significant role in working for religious freedom in the Iron Curtain countries, more than many people recognize.

Maurice Rowlandson   I was one of the people, along with Walter Smyth and Dr. Alexander Haraszti, who he consulted about going to the Soviet Union. I told him he should go. He was worried that his first visit to the Soviet Union was on this conference for the establishment of peace among the peoples of Europe. I said, "Billy, you can still preach the Gospel. You can talk about peace with God."

From the very beginning, his prayer was that he might be able to preach the Gospel in Moscow. How he got there was through the back door, as it were, going to Hungary, Bulgaria, and Romania and opening a door through which Dr. Haraszti carefully and skillfully maneuvered with the help of Smyth and another Graham associate, John Akers.

———

To some people, Graham paid too high a price for his opportunity to preach in the Soviet Union and other Eastern European nations. His critics believe that he had compromised his integrity, even negatively affecting U.S. policy goals vis-à-vis the Soviet Union. Graham's reaction to those assertions was both predictable and honest: "I know I may be used for propaganda . . . but I believe my propaganda— the Gospel of Christ—is stronger."

China, 1988, 1992, and 1994

In 1980, Ruth Graham made a sentimental visit to the town where she had grown up. The visit led to an invitation from the China Christian Council and the Chinese People's Association for Friendship with Foreign countries (respectively, a government-approved and a governmental body) for her husband, who had wanted to visit China ever since meeting Ruth at Wheaton College. He was to go there in the fall of 1987.

As far as he was concerned, China, with its population of more than one billion people, was the hub of the increasingly important "Pacific Rim." It was also one of the few major nations where he had not preached the Gospel. At the same time, China retained its communist ideology and—as was the case following his initial visit to the Soviet Union—Graham knew he would be attacked by elements of the religious and political right, as well as by organizations and individuals concerned over China's abysmal record on human rights. Following a spirited discussion with their associates concerning whether they should accept the Chinese invitation, Graham decided it was an opportunity not to be missed.

The visit was put off until the following April, however, because he fell and broke several ribs.

———

Henry Holley   I was involved in the decision to go to China, and I was with Mr. Graham in Tokyo in 1988 when he fell and broke his rib and we had to delay the trip. When I told [Irvin] Shorty Yeaworth, the project director for the trip, that Mr. Graham could not go, Shorty had a hard time with that news. He said, "He's *got* to go." And I said, "Shorty, you don't hear me. He's broken his rib and cannot go."

In the meantime, in preparing for their trip Billy and Ruth sought the advice of a number of China experts, including Sidney Rittenberg, an academician and business consultant who had gone to China in 1946 as an idealistic young university graduate. There, although Rittenberg established a friendship with the Chinese leader, Mao Zedong, he was arrested on suspicion of spying. He was released, only to be imprisoned again during the Cultural Revolution; he spent sixteen years in Chinese prisons.

Sidney Rittenberg   Aside from being a great evangelist, he is a great American—he represents the best in American values. He does not allow himself to be placed on a pedestal. Before we went to China with Billy and Ruth in 1988, we attended his crusade in Denver. There he spent a great deal of time telling his audience that they must not assume that the evangelist is closer to God than they are. He told them that the evangelist is like a beggar who finds a crust of bread and then tells other beggars where they can find it.

The Question of Whether Graham Should Even Go There

Henry Holley   Billy will feel like he has a position, but he will seek counsel from others. Not just people who would say yes, but people whose opinion he values. In the case of China, as everywhere else, he goes where he has been invited. He didn't just decide to go to China; that visit was the result of a cultivation process, an invitation, and then an acceptance.

Sidney Rittenberg   In the meetings concerning whether he should go to China or not, Billy met with State Department officials, journalists, all sorts of advisers, and some of his own people. Most of them were not really in favor of his going. At the final meeting, held in his home in Montreat, the State Department official present very solemnly counseled him that if he did go to China and meet with government leaders, he shouldn't talk to them about Jesus and about Christianity because they would be offended. Billy didn't respond, but in a break in the discussion he came over to me and my wife, Yulin, and asked what we thought about that. I said, "If you go to China and don't talk about Jesus, they won't believe you're Billy Graham. They will expect you to talk about what you have always talked about." So he did, and it went very well.

At the same session, one of the American correspondents who had been stationed in Beijing said, "You know, when you go there they will invite you to preach in a hall with two hundred people, and one hundred and eighty of them will be police agents." Billy has such wisdom; he immediately said, "Oh, I'd love to preach to them. They are the ones who really need it."

Betty Bao Lord If people in China weren't Christians, or cognizant of what was happening in America, they would not generally have been aware of Mr. Graham's visit.

Sidney Rittenberg Ruth, who is more politically conservative than Billy, said, "Well I suppose if the Lord waited until everything was fine on earth before He sent His Son down, He probably never would have sent Him." That closed the discussion on whether they should go to China.

Winston Lord They probably wouldn't have welcomed Mr. Graham in the first place if they had thought he was going to be a flame-thrower. His reputation for tolerance preceded him and they recognized that he probably wouldn't do anything that would be awkward for them. They probably saw this as a modest opportunity to demonstrate flexibility and to gain public relations points by welcoming him.

The First Visit

Sidney Rittenberg In 1988, on Billy's first trip to China, we were ushered into an airport VIP room after landing in Beijing. For the first five minutes, the Chinese officials in the room and the Graham party sat around looking uncomfortable, not knowing what to say beyond formalities. But soon Billy had them relaxed and laughing; it was a totally different atmosphere. A few days after we arrived, the American ambassador, Winston Lord, hosted a luncheon at the embassy. Included among the guests was the head of the body that manages religious affairs for the Central Committee.

Winston Lord   The luncheon was at the embassy residence with about twelve to fifteen guests. It was a modest size that encouraged roundtable discussion, so we could have a collective discussion. We had people from the church hierarchy in China and a couple of people engaged in political reform—nobody radical, just people interested in human rights and religion. Betty, who had many contacts among reformers and academics, including cultural areas, came up with some names and I would consult with my embassy colleagues who followed the areas of politics and religion, and a couple of people from my staff, as well.

Sidney Rittenberg   At the end of a two-hour discussion, the vice-foreign minister offered a toast in which he said, "The spirit of Karl Marx and the spirit of Jesus Christ have been with us in this room." That was a remarkable thing for an old Chinese communist to say.

Meetings with the Chinese Leadership

Sidney Rittenberg   The main thing that Billy and Mao Zedong have in common is that they are both very famous. Mao talked of, and constantly wrote about, the dangers of arrogance and being corrupted by power. And yet for all his preaching he was probably more corrupted by power than most people in history. And here's Billy Graham, who has had every opportunity to get rich, to throw his weight around, to become very arrogant, and he never has.

The meeting with the premier, Li Peng, a rather stiff man, was fairly formal but quite friendly. Billy advised him to read something about the life of Christ; not as religion but as the story of a man who has had such a tremendous influence down through history. The premier looked at me as though to say, My, what a curious thing to utter.

Taking Risks to Spread the Gospel

Sidney Rittenberg   Billy preached in many different Chinese churches, including some home churches not recognized by the government, and he had a tremendous reception everywhere. Billy wanted to visit a retired minister who had been in prison for many years and now lived in Shanghai, providing it would not offend our hosts. So I asked the government official who was in charge of our trip, and he said, "Please tell Dr. Graham that he is perfectly free to go anywhere he wants, as long as he doesn't *ask* me."

A Moving Visit to Ruth Bell Graham's Childhood Home

Betty Bao Lord   Mrs. Graham's birth in China, and her previous history in China, was of great interest to everyone. That was sort of a door opener for everybody to be very warm to them. Of course, they are wonderful people, so that came across. It was an important visit because Mr. Graham was probably one of the first religious leaders in the United States to go there.

Sidney Rittenberg   It was very moving when we arrived in Ruth's home town. When we got there the mayor, who happened to be a woman, and what looked like the whole population of the town turned out to meet us at the town's entrance. When we went to the main square, a number of elderly people came up to Ruth and took her by the hand and told her that her father [Dr. L. Nelson Bell] had brought them into the world. And we saw that her father's hospital was still functioning.

Winston Lord   The overall impression of this couple is a very positive one, of course. I have always admired them from a distance and we came away feeling great respect and affection for both of them. It wasn't just Billy; they are a team. It made you proud that they were Americans. They conducted themselves with great courtesy and effectiveness. It was a very positive experience for us.

Returning to China

Sidney Rittenberg   In 1992, when we met with the vice premier—he later became premier—the session was warm and affectionate. Billy gave him a copy of a Chinese Bible that he had inscribed, and after thanking him the vice premier told Billy that he had a copy of the Bible in English in his home. He said that he read from this Bible from time to time because "we need to know the best of the cultures of all countries, not just our own."

The Koreas

Graham first traveled to the Korean peninsula in 1950, at Christmas time. There he preached to U.S. troops from a specially built platform, met with individual soldiers, and visited field hospitals close to the front. He returned to South Korea in 1956, to preach and meet with young people. Then in 1973 he held a major crusade in Seoul.

———————

South Korea, 1973

Henry Holley   I was the crusade director in South Korea in 1973. Times have changed. In Seoul, I had one manual typewriter in my office. Now we have computers and other equipment to help us do the job. We do the same job as back then; it's just that we have the technology to do things more and better and faster, with more accuracy, perhaps. Today, I tell young crusade directors, "Look, when I first started, we were typing mailing lists using carbon paper" (they didn't know what carbon paper was) "and we'd make five or six carbon sets and then take scissors and cut out the labels and keep labels for a second and third mailing." They couldn't get over that.

I asked Billy Kim to be Dr. Graham's interpreter. That was quite a struggle for him because he was from a church that did not altogether agree with Billy Graham. Billy Kim had a real decision to make, but he made the *right* decision.

Billy Kim   We would meet each day at 2:00 P.M. in his hotel room to go over his sermon. At the team breakfast before the Crusade began, Mr. Graham said, "We are reaping; we haven't done any work here. The Korean Christians have worked and prayed." I think the team was surprised at how many people, many of whom had walked for miles, came to the meetings. We started at half a million and then went to 650,000, then 750,000, then 850,000 and, on the final day, that remarkable crowd of 1.1 million people. The [public's] response was due to several factors: first, the notoriety of Billy Graham. Second, Korea was ripe because we had a strong totalitarian government at that time. The president, [Chung Hee] Park, was very interested in all phases of the welfare of the Korean people, including the spiritual. At that time, we faced a constant threat from North Korea, and the army chief of staff told the military: one man, one faith—whether you are a Buddhist, a Catholic, a Protestant, every soldier should have one faith. This he believed would make for better, stronger soldiers. Third, the Korean Church was at work evangelizing the nation. So in 1973 it all came together as God brought such a magnitude of a crowd from all over Korea.

Everyone on the Crusade committee was surprised at the size of the crowd on the last day [estimated at 1.1 million]. Mr. Graham had to leave immediately after the service, and as he and T. W. Wilson circled the grounds in a helicopter provided by the U.S. Army, everyone waved their programs. It felt like Jesus was ascending up to heaven.

Henry Holley   We had a cumulative total of 3.2 million people in five days; the closing day was 1.1 million people. The venue, Yoido Plaza, had been an airstrip during the Korean War. It was a mile long and one-half mile wide, and we had built the platform—the size of a two-story building—in the middle of the Plaza. The people were seated on the tarmac as far as the eye could see. The organizers had painted squares on the asphalt tarmac; each one held two thousand people and that is how they tabulated the attendance. I had made arrangements for the U.S. Army to provide a helicopter to fly Billy from the back of the platform to Kimpo Airport as it would have been impossible to drive an automobile through the crowd. As we flew over the vast crowd and saw the people waving their handkerchiefs at us, we were overwhelmed with the enormity of the crowd. We had never seen so many people before gathered in one place; it looked like an anthill. That last day was quite an experience.

In what was likely the most unusual trip of his career, Billy at the age of seventy-four flew from the relatively benign atmosphere of Beijing to the forbidding precincts of Pyongyang, the capital of North Korea. His official invitation came from the Korean Christians Federation and the Korean Catholics Association (Protestant and Roman Catholic organizations, respectively).

North Korea, 1992

Henry Holley   After the Hong Kong Crusade in 1990, where I was the Crusade director, I was in Billy's room talking about every place in Asia where we had been together, where I had prepared meetings for him. He said, "Well, we've been everywhere in Asia, haven't we?" I replied, "Not really, Billy." He asked, "Where's that?" And I said, "Pyongyang, North Korea." He was so thrilled; he said, "You know, Ruth went to school there. Do you think we could ever get into North Korea?" I answered that I wasn't sure but that I would cultivate the possibility. For the next year, I worked on securing an invitation through Ho Jong, the North Korean ambassador at the United Nations. Over a period of time, he invited us to make an exploratory trip. I hired Steve Linton, who was an associate professor of Korean studies at Columbia University, to be our counselor and interpreter.

Dale Kietzman   We were the guests of the former North Korean ambassador to the United Nations at a dinner in Pyongyang. In the course of the conversation, he was asking how they could persuade the American public that they weren't the terrible people that they felt they were being portrayed as. I suggested that Americans needed to see for themselves; therefore they ought to open the country for tourism. He told me that they were not yet quite ready for that. I said, "Well, I guess you will have to invite some representative people." He answered that they had done that but without success. I asked who he had invited and he mentioned Joan Baez, Ramsey Clark, and perhaps one or two others. I said, "They are the wrong people to invite; you need to have people from the center—the evangelical center of the American public." He asked who I meant, and the first name I came up with was Billy Graham. We were seated at a large round table, and no one other than the ambassador had ever heard of Billy Graham.

Henry Holley   In visiting North Korea, we had three objectives: one was to have Billy speak in the churches, the second was to meet with Kim Il Sung, and third to have Billy speak to the faculty and students at Kim Il Sung University. They met all three of those requests. That was the beginning of a good friendship.

———————

Writing in the introduction to *North Korean Journey,* a book issued by the BGEA's World Wide Publications, Graham characterized his trip to the Democratic People's Republic of Korea as "undoubtedly one of the most memorable visits I have ever made to any country." Then, stating that going there was the fulfillment of his and Ruth's dream, Graham wrote, "Across the years I had also developed a personal concern about the situation in the Korean peninsula. . . . I longed to have fellowship with my fellow Christian believers in North Korea, and also to make whatever contribution I could to better understanding and good will."

———————

Stephen Linton   Mr. Graham had expressed an interest in visiting North Korea and some of his associates were looking for a way that he might go; some of them had not worked out. In a meeting in Montreat, Mr. Graham had mentioned his interest in going to Korea to an ex-missionary, who said, "You should get in touch with Steve Linton." Then two of Mr. Graham's associates, Dr. John Akers and Henry Holley, came to see me in New York, and we worked together off and on for the next ten years.

Dale Kietzman   I had been back in California for a month or so when I received a call saying that they would like to invite Billy Graham, but they wanted to make sure that he would respond to an invitation. I called the Graham headquarters and spoke to the executive director of the ministry, who told me, "I don't have to ask Billy Graham that because we had a staff meeting this past week and we were asking him where he would like to minister in the time he's got left and he replied, 'One country: North Korea.' So he will respond."

Getting There

Stephen Linton   I am certain that the North Korean officials knew that Mr. Graham had conducted crusades in South Korea, and I would imagine that they knew he had been there in 1950. The fact that Mrs. Graham had attended school in Pyongyang was front and center from the beginning, starting with the negotiations with the North Korean diplomats in New York; it created a potential bond. I am sure that the North Koreans knew of Mr. Graham's anticommunism earlier in his career, but they are not as exclusively ideological as one might think. If someone is polite and willing to be gracious, they are willing to overlook an awful lot that might surprise you.

From Graham's Perspective

Stephen Linton   Mr. Graham vets trips extensively. We took three preparatory trips for his first visit to North Korea. Ned Graham and Mrs. Graham went, as did Franklin. I imagine I have been to North Korea for the Grahams about ten times over a ten-year period. Mr. Graham wants to put his best foot forward, to make a good impression as a Christian leader, to encourage more positive visibility for the church, and he succeeded in doing that. He was not there to pressure the North Korean government but to encourage it and to offer his personal friendship to their leadership, and his good wishes to their people and his blessings on their society.

———————

On Graham's arrival at Kim Il Sung International Airport, he said, "I have come to this country for the same reasons I have visited many other countries across the world. As Christ's ambassador, I have come first of all to visit the Christian community here—to have fellowship with my brothers and sisters in Christ, to pray and to worship with them, and to preach the Gospel of Jesus Christ in your churches."

Graham also suggested that he had come to North Korea with an additional agenda, observing that "the DPRK and the United States are not natural enemies. It is past time that the suspicion and enmity which have characterized our relations for the last half century were replaced with trust and friendship. I pray that this trip may be a positive step in that direction."

The North Koreans' View of Graham

Stephen Linton   The North Koreans were curious; they didn't quite know what to make of Mr. Graham's interest in visiting their country. Frankly, they had not heard much about Mr. Graham. I venture to say that North Koreans as a people knew less about Mr. Graham when he began his relationship with them than any other peoples he had visited. On the other hand, North Koreans are always looking for interesting opportunities—at least at that time—to introduce [the late] Kim Il Sung to foreigners whom he would find interesting and who, arguably, would not embarrass them. Mr. Graham certainly looked like a good candidate. They were also interested in an opening to the U.S., as they still are to some extent, and it was his prominence in American society that made him an obvious choice on that account as well.

Recruiting Interpreters

Dwight Linton   My nephew, who was working with the team and doing much of the negotiating, asked me to serve as a translator. Steve did more translating than I did; whenever there was an official meeting, my nephew had that vocabulary much better than I do. The Billy Graham team decided that for the preaching that he did, he needed to have a Korean speaker who could translate from the English into Korean, but the North Koreans would not allow an English-speaking South Korean to participate, and that meant that Mr. Graham would have to get a speaker from the Anglo or missionary community. I was available at the time and my age helped me; the Koreans will let an older person get away with a lot of mistakes.

Arranging a Meeting between the Evangelist and the Paramount Leader

Dwight Linton   We were staying at a beautiful guest house that had been built by the communist government. While a meeting with the Great Leader [as Kim Il Sung was variously called, another of his titles having been Paramount Leader] was not part of our schedule, there was some indication that we might meet with him.

Stephen Linton   You could not "book" Kim Il Sung in advance. You could express a desire and a hope that it would take place, but meetings at that level were not set up in advance. Mr. Graham would have considered the trip a failure if he hadn't met Kim Il Sung. Mr. Graham was put up in a guest house, and we had a series of meetings with the foreign minister and with Catholic and Protestant church leaders, as well as banquets and press conferences. Toward the end of the trip, officials said, "We have good news; the meeting will happen." We met with Kim Il Sung in one of his dachas on the outskirts of the city, and there he was, waiting to say hi to us at the door, where he gave Mr. Graham a big hug.

Henry Holley   Kim Il Sung invited us to lunch; it was quite an experience. The meeting with him was set in concrete; that was part of the conditions of our coming. The chemistry was quite interesting. It was—pardon the expression—two old men, two grandfathers meeting together. Kim Il Sung did quite a few evil things in his time, but one-on-one it was a very cordial first meeting. Billy gave him a Bible as well as a porcelain swan. The president unexpectedly invited the small party that accompanied Billy to have lunch with him. The president sat to my right and Billy sat to the president's right. During the course of the meal a very interesting thing happened. With his chopsticks, Kim Il Sung would pick up a morsel from a common plate and put it on Billy's plate and he did the same to mine. I knew the culture well enough to understand that that was a very high gesture—a communication that we had favor with him.

The conversation was very fluid; we talked about springtime, about the weather. We were not naïve; we knew they wanted Billy Graham, a high-profile religious figure who had good connections with the White House and the political scene in America. They wanted him to come because they were looking for someone to help them achieve diplomatic relations with the United States. They probably wanted to exploit Billy. But they didn't have that opportunity; Billy was too wise.

Dwight Linton   On Thursday morning, our group was called together, and you could feel the tension rising. His [Kim Il Sung's] private home was about twenty miles outside of Pyongyang. It was a huge house; on one wall there was a huge painting. He and Billy had a private discussion, and then there was picture taking. We all sat down at a large round table and Billy Graham sat next to the Great Leader. At that point, the Great Leader led the conversation, and I was greatly impressed by his charisma. It was a very friendly interchange. I do not think he understood very well what Dr. Graham represented. I believe he learned a good deal during that time, and on the next trip [in 1994] they spent a lot of relaxed time together.

The general conversation in that first meeting was interesting. You can imagine what kind of an ego Kim Il Sung had. So much of the conversation related to things he had been able to do. They had developed a mythology about him, and he contributed to that. For example, he said, "They all told me you could not raise oriental pears in North Korea because it is too cold. But I saw some in China, and I told my people what to do, and now we can raise these pears." He had another story about rainbow trout. He was very outgoing, the kind of a person that draws other people. That to me was the explanation of how he stayed in his position for fifty or so years as leader of the people of North Korea.

Dale Kietzman   I got indirect feedback concerning the fact that he was able to speak to Kim Il Sung—which I did not have the privilege of doing—and my contacts were very pleased at the exposure American television gave to the visit. That was the best coverage they'd had.

Henry Holley   In Pyongyang, Billy stated that he was not a politician and that he had not come representing his government but had come as a citizen of his government. He said that he was a citizen of the Kingdom of Heaven and a minister of the Gospel. To this day, we enjoy good relations with the officials in the Democratic People's Republic of Korea. I have met the foreign minister as well as all of the members of the presidium. The motivation for us to maintain good relations is that someday God is going to open the doors to North Korea and we are going to be in a position to proclaim the Gospel. My prayer is that there will be a peaceful unification between North and South Korea.

The Evangelist Preaches—North Korean Style

Dwight Linton   When we got to the church everyone was in their seat, sitting quietly at the time the meeting was scheduled to start. When I relate this to Korean audiences in the United States, they laugh because you cannot normally get Koreans to church on time.

I translated for him at the Pongsu church—the Protestant church—and at the Catholic church. On these visits, you get very little time to talk to ordinary people. It's been over ten years since Dr. Graham's first trip, and I am still wondering who the people in attendance at his meetings were. The people were very attentive, but the question is, How can they live as Christians in that situation? We didn't have a chance to talk with them individually; the officials do not give us that freedom. There are some theories; one is that they are the children of Christians. Pyongyang had a very high percentage of Christians, perhaps one-tenth of the city's population. When we go today to the two Protestant churches, they have choirs that sing beautifully. As far as we can determine, the hymns they sing came from pre-war Korea, so you have the Gospel very clearly sung in the hymns. We ask ourselves: Who *are* these people? What do they do for a living? The church very definitely is not allowed to do anything outside of what we see there. It may be that the government sends out an order saying, Today you show up in church. I think it is more complex. I am convinced it's not just a bunch of people who are responding to a government order; I believe that those people have decided they want to be Christians and have so persuaded the government.

The Catholic Church is trying to secure recognition from the pope. You have to realize that the preachers are all paid by the government. At the Catholic church, they did not have a service and have Billy Graham preach. They said, You can't do that. Instead the priest got up and preached a sermon which was just pure and simple propaganda. They closed the service with a benediction and then they allowed Billy Graham to have a lecture. Billy was humble. He didn't complain about that put-down; he just went right on through with his routine and preached his sermon.

Graham Carries a Presidential Message

Stephen Linton   Mr. Graham and Kim Il Sung hit it off very well. Kim Il Sung found him charming; they discussed many subjects for a long, long time and had dinner together. It was an occasion that both of them seemed to enjoy. There wasn't a lot of negotiation; Mr. Graham doesn't do that, understandably so. He's there to spread goodwill. But on both of his visits he did carry presidential messages. He delivered them and took back some reactions.

1994

Stephen Linton   Mr. Graham's trip in 1994, which took place at an extremely cold period of the year, was an expression of concern for the deteriorating relations between the U.S. and North Korea. There was a face-to-face meeting with only the foreign minister and me present, in addition to the two men. The son [Kim Jong Il] was not in on the meetings; it would have been bad form on the part of the North Koreans to have the son watching over Daddy doing his thing, and Kim Jong Il was very adept at being a filial son.

Henry Holley   The father was the undisputed leader. No one was going to compete with him before he died.

Stephen Linton   At the time, this was under a Democratic administration [the Clinton years] when, at least as officials report now, there were reports that a strike against North Korea's nuclear facility was contemplated. There was a good deal of saber rattling on both sides. Mr. Graham made a special effort not to mediate or to negotiate in lieu of anybody but simply to express his concern, to deliver a message from then–President Clinton, and to renew the friendship. This was extremely well received by the North Koreans because he was not in good health and he had come in a very cold part of the year; obviously he wasn't on a sightseeing trip. He had no personal agenda, but just to express well wishes and concern for the situation. It is hard to overemphasize the impression it made.

Ruth Graham and Her Children Return to the Scene of Her School Years

Henry Holley   Mrs. Graham was there. She has a real heart for Korea and was delighted to be back on the Korean peninsula. She greatly supported and encouraged her husband. I had organized several ladies' events for her. The senior members of the crusade committee had originally come from North Korea, so they had a real joy in their heart when they saw Ruth.

Stephen Linton   Franklin and Gigi went with Mrs. Graham after Kim Il Sung passed away. It was made very clear to them that this was a response on Kim Jong Il's part, an attempt to honor the friendship between the Grahams and his father. Franklin never met Kim Jong Il, which, I believe, was a disappointment. Ruth, who was accompanied by her daughter, Gigi, wanted to see the sights of Pyongyang, particularly the school she had attended.

Dwight Linton   I attended that school for six weeks in 1940; I was in the eighth grade. Then, in November, all of the American missionaries left Korea and the school was closed and never reopened. It was a boarding school basically designed for missionary kids. There were fifty to seventy students, and the teachers came from the States. I grew up in Chunju, a small village in the far south, and I really looked forward to attending the school and was very disappointed when I had to leave. In my town, we could do a little ice skating, but the river there didn't stay frozen very long. I was looking forward to the ice skating that you could do on the Potong River in Pyongyang. The ice would be several feet thick and would stay frozen all winter long.

Stephen Linton   The Grahams' visits were treated as head-of-state visits. The reception they received was uncommon. Ned Graham visited several times, acting as his father's envoy.

The Aftermath of their Visits

Stephen Linton   Mr. Graham's visits to the North were a very sensitive issue in South Korea. There were people who tried to dissuade him. After the first visit, when they saw the positive effect, some of that concern dissipated.

Dwight Linton   I believe that the most important impact of Billy Graham's trips is that the Great Leader had never met Westerners. He was probably full of suspicion that they were going to try to use the visit to undermine him. He was initially tense and then gradually melted. I have talked to Steve about the second trip, and he said those two men just sat down like two old grandfathers and talked. What happened was that Billy Graham became an icon to all of the next echelon of leadership. Because of that, quite a few NGOs [nongovernmental organizations] have been able to get into North Korea and do various kinds of work there. I believe Dr. Graham's visits had a very real impact upon that side of things; they had an effect which made it easier for Jimmy Carter to go in and negotiate.

Henry Holley   I know that Jimmy Carter's visit was an outcome of Mr. Graham's visit. The Carter people called me after our visit to North Korea in 1992, seeking advice on North Korea.

Stephen Linton   I wouldn't say that Jimmy Carter's trip to North Korea was a direct result of Billy Graham's visits, but it certainly prepared the way for a visit by a former president. I believe Mr. Graham briefed Mr. Carter. From the North Koreans' perspective, Billy Graham was probably the first American of a nonideological persuasion who had offered them friendship in an unqualified way and had also shown due respect for their society and people in a way that very few people in America do. President Carter is someone—this is typical of American reaction to North Korea—who doesn't emphasize as much as Mr. Graham did the development and maintaining of a relationship. He wants to fix problems— I did some informal consulting for him as well. He made one trip and Mr. Graham made two. President Carter was available to solve problems; he was not there to become a friend. There is an enormous difference in the way that is perceived in North Korea; it's much less productive to take an engineer's approach versus a pastoral approach.

Dale Kietzman   There may not have been long-range benefit from Mr. Graham's visit because with the death of Kim Il Sung all things have changed. If Kim Il Sung had continued to live, there would have been a third trip; I understand it was planned. His son is entirely different.

––––––––––

In addition to undertaking his visits to China, North Korea, and the Soviet Union, from 1982 to 1994 Graham held crusades and meetings in more than fifty cities in the United States, the United Kingdom, and Europe. As important as those events were, it appeared that his ministry was reaching a new plateau from which he would be recognized as a man determined to facilitate achievement of both peace and international understanding.

Israel

One area of the world that was of special theological interest to Graham was the Middle East. As a student of the Scriptures committed to a premillennial understanding of Christ's Second Coming—a major focus of his preaching—Graham carefully followed political developments that affected the State of Israel.

Prior to 1977, his contacts with Israeli leaders were limited to officials representing the ruling Labor Party. In May of that year, Menachem Begin, the fabled leader of the underground Irgun Zvai Leumi movement, became prime minister when his Likud Party bested Labor in a national election. The world media lost no time in demonizing Begin, characterizing him as a fanatic or worse. *Time* magazine went further, running an anti-Semitically tinged headline, "Begin, as in

Fagin," in reference to Dickens's unsavory character in *Oliver Twist,* who just happened to be Jewish. (In response, the editor of the *New York Jewish Week* ran the headline, "*Time* Rhymes with Slime.")

Begin was able to put together a basically right-wing government, one committed to Jewish settlement of the Biblical heartlands of Judea and Samaria. Unlike his predecessors, he was not fearful of developing strong relationships with the thirty-million-strong U.S. evangelical community, because he realized the political potential of the friendship and support of so many Americans who shared his belief in Israel's right to its ancient Biblical patrimony.

Gerald Strober   During those years, I served as Begin's unofficial adviser on the evangelical community, and in that capacity I arranged many meetings between him or his close associates with American evangelical leaders. Billy, like many other American religious leaders, had never met Begin, and while having read all the negative media reports about him he wanted to make his own judgment. And so when I called Billy to inform him that Shmuel Katz, Begin's former underground comrade—he had served on the Irgun's High Command and was now the prime minister's cabinet-level adviser on overseas information—was coming to the United States, he asked me to bring Katz to Cincinnati, where a crusade was in progress.

I sat in on the two-hour meeting as a kind of fly on the wall and listened as Katz briefed Billy on the prime minister's personality and program. It was a fascinating discussion. Billy asked pointed and informed questions, and it was obvious that he held Israel's well-being close to his heart. At the same time, Billy has always had to balance his positive feelings for the Jewish State with concern for ordinary Arabs caught up in the Israeli-Palestinian conflict.

In any consideration of Israel, one must take into account the Jewish communities of the diaspora. Thus, in addition to Graham's theological views and practical concerns for the Jewish State, he has always sought to relate to the American Jewish community.

Graham's Strong Feelings for the Jewish People

Gerald Strober   He truly believes that God has a special relationship with the Jewish people, a view that he expressed at length to me and to Rabbi Tanenbaum when we visited his home in 1972. On that occasion,

Ruth Graham had prepared a special luncheon, one that was much more elaborate than the soup and crackers the Grahams normally had at mid-day. When we came to the table, Ruth told us she had broiled filet mignon. "Oh," said Rabbi Tanenbaum, "I cannot eat unkosher meat." Ruth, who had assumed that the rabbi would be able to eat any meat other than *pork,* was crushed. And I was amazed, as I had traveled exten-sively with Marc Tanenbaum and believed that he *did* eat nonkosher meat. In that instance, it was obvious that the rabbi did not realize that he had embarrassed his lovely and sincere hostess, who had tried so hard to do the right thing.

Graham's Initial Outreach to the American Jewish Community

Gerald Strober   In late 1968, following a year of research on the man-ner in which Christian Sunday School materials treated Jews and Judaism, I was invited to join the Interreligious Affairs staff of the American Jewish Committee, whose main office is located on East 56th Street in Manhattan. I was to encourage the various Protestant denomi-nations involved in the study to implement its recommendations. At that time, the man I worked under, Rabbi Marc H. Tanenbaum—he had made great strides in relating to the Vatican and the Catholic hierarchy in the United States—wanted to broaden the committee's scope by becoming involved with the evangelical community, and I was given the assignment of beginning to make that happen.

For the next five years, along with Rabbi Tanenbaum and my colleague and close friend, Rabbi A. James Rudin, I was involved in organizing meetings between evangelical and Jewish scholars. One memorable col-loquium took place at Southern Baptist Theological Seminary, in Louisville, Kentucky, where for the first time ever Jewish and Southern Baptist theologians, rabbis, and ministers grappled in a tense but friendly encounter with the weighty issues of mission and conversion. In partici-pants' minds was the realization that Billy Graham, then at the height of his fame and influence, was a member of a Southern Baptist congrega-tion, the First Baptist Church of Dallas.

In addition to my other responsibilities on the committee, I began to develop relationships with both Billy and his close associate, T. W. Wilson. In 1969, Billy visited the committee's headquarters, where he met with a group of Jewish leaders. The committee's president, Morris

Abram, a distinguished attorney who had an excellent Jewish education and was often invited to speak in Baptist churches (he had also been an aide to President Kennedy), told the evangelist of his own boyhood, spent in Fitzgerald, Georgia. Abram and Billy got along famously, their rich southern cadences pleasing to the guests assembled in the committee's large conference room.

At that time, I would travel once or twice yearly to a Graham crusade. In places like Knoxville, Detroit, and Atlanta, I would have private meetings with the evangelist, spending forty-five minutes to an hour briefing him on the latest developments in Israel. In 1971, World Wide Pictures, the film-making arm of the BGEA, released *His Land,* an hour-long documentary shot in Israel that strongly made the case for the Jewish people's claim to their ancient homeland.

The American Jewish Committee welcomed the film, which would eventually be screened in thousands of churches. I prepared a study guide to accompany the film, and the committee assisted the BGEA in promoting its release. While the film uncompromisingly presented the dispensationalist view of Christ's return and its aftermath—a contentious subject today between evangelicals and some Jews—it did so in a loving manner. And while most contemporary films about Israel depict the reborn nation in harsh terms—the result, perhaps, of a certain brand of political correctness in which it is considered "evenhanded" to characterize the Jewish State as an aggressor nation—*His Land* was a celebration of Israeli life in the halcyon days following the Six Day War, which took place in June 1967.

———————

Graham's long and honorable relationship with the Jewish community was severely tested when in 2002 the National Archives released a tape of a conversation he had years earlier with then-President Nixon. In that discussion, the president referred to his opponents in the American Jewish community, particularly those in the media. At one point, Graham interjected, "This stranglehold [in the American media] has got to be broken or the country's going down the drain."

———————

Dwight Chapin   What rings true with me would be Nixon's very pro stance on Israel. Yet the *New York Times* and its ownership would be all over him despite the fact that he had been doing yeoman work for the Jewish community vis-à-vis Israel. I know that Nixon had problems—that

they would beat the hell out of him constantly, whereas he was really trying to do a lot to help Israel. That was the heart of the matter. Now how
Billy gets into the middle of this is mind-boggling. Maybe he was trying to
say things that he thought the president would want to hear. I just can't
explain it. What I do know is that the president would have trouble with
some of the media ownership or control when it would come to issues
that were affecting Israel. Nixon helped Israel because he thought he was
doing the right thing; he didn't do it to get support from the *New York
Times*. He was not a fool; he knew very well what they felt about him. But
it would get his goat occasionally. He was not under any false illusions; it
just *upset* him.

Gerald Strober   I vividly recall a conversation with Billy when he, with
no little perplexity, remarked that he was shocked by the fact that the *New
York Times* did not demonstrate more support for Israel. I informed him
that the newspaper had historically opposed the Zionist movement and
only grudgingly accepted the founding of the Jewish State in 1948. In the
intervening years, the publication's editorials suggested that Israel's territory be limited to the coastal plain along the Mediterranean Sea. Such a
concept was foreign to Billy, and most evangelicals, who understood the
Jewish patrimony to include the regions of Judea and Samaria [the West
Bank], and all of Jerusalem.

When the tape was made public, Graham at first said that he could not recall the
conversation. Later, in a statement, he wrote of those interjected words: "They do
not reflect my views and I sincerely apologize for any offense caused by the
remarks. . . . I cannot imagine what caused me to make those comments. . . . I
was wrong for not disagreeing with the president. My remarks did not reflect my
love for the Jewish people. I humbly ask the Jewish community to reflect on
my actions on behalf of Jews over the years that contradict my words in the Oval
Office that day."

Gerald Strober   At that time, I exchanged letters with Billy, who was
quite upset concerning what the Jewish community would now likely
think of him. He closely monitored the Jewish press—I sent him a number of clippings and his personal assistant found others—describing the
community's reactions to his words. On March 22, 2002, Billy wrote to

me, "How thoughtful of you to call me after the Nixon tape story appeared, and the various articles and statements. Thank you for wanting to be a friendly voice from the past to encourage me."

Though some Jews hastily decided that Graham's comment to Nixon was a true reflection of his attitude, many others, reflecting on both the evangelist's record of support for Israel and his friendly relations with Jewish organizations and individuals, gave him the benefit of the doubt. William Martin, Graham's authorized biographer, told *Christianity Today* that since the tapes often contained gaps, this particular conversation does not clearly demonstrate whether the evangelist was concerned about Jews generally or more specifically about Jewish liberals. As Martin stated, "[Graham] frequently showed some tendency to want to agree with those he was with, particularly those in power."

Graham continued to make amends to the American Jewish community. In Cincinnati, just prior to the beginning of his Crusade there in June 2002, he met with Jewish leaders and once again apologized for having spoken negatively to Nixon about Jews so many years earlier.

Gerald Strober   I trust that Professor Martin had it right: that Billy does tend to agree with people in power. Whether that has been a conscious tactic, a *quid pro quo* to enable him to influence political leaders by agreeing with their views and obviously their prejudices, or whether he just likes to ingratiate himself with powerful people, is difficult to judge. Whatever the reason for that unfortunate interjection, one can be certain that Billy would give up much to be able to take it back. My sense is that he understood Nixon only too well and that those words did not reflect his true feelings about Jews. Rather, he was patronizing his patron of the moment.

I do know that when I visited Billy at his home in the early spring of 1975, he expressed shock at what tapes released in the wake of the Watergate investigation had revealed concerning Nixon's many profanities. Billy claimed then that the chameleonlike former president had never used such crude language during their many conversations, and he suggested that one reason for Nixon's emotional outbursts, as well as his post-Watergate break-in actions, may have been due to his use of strong prescription drugs. As Billy spoke, I was convinced that he felt betrayed by Nixon, a man to whom he had extended friendship and with whom he had become so closely identified.

Dwight Chapin   That language is not unlike if you were sitting in the director's truck when they were doing Monday Night Football. You hear a lot of that kind of stuff; I have been in countless business meetings where people let out with that kind of profanity. But nobody is about to do it if the Right Reverend Somebody is standing there. It takes on a different atmosphere because of the person present. That could also have been [with] a woman; I defy you to find any tape of Nixon where he would have used that kind of language had a woman been present in the Oval Office. He would not have done that with Billy Graham or the Greek archbishop or some rabbi; his language would be cleaned up for those occasions.

Chapter Seven

THE NEW EVANGELICALISM

Leighton Ford Billy was not the only one who was espousing this [new evangelicalism], but he symbolized the movement in a very significant way. He was able to bridge both the world of evangelism and the world of evangelical theology in a way that I don't think anybody else was doing at that time. Even though he was not himself a theologian—in fact he felt very inadequate theologically—he understood the importance of thinking and having intellectual weight to the faith. In that way, he brought those worlds together. Billy's pulling together of popular evangelism and its strong spiritual emphasis of calling people to Christ with an appreciation for adding intellectual weight to it were very important.

Taking Issue with Graham

David Epstein There have been people who have taken issue with him on secondary matters, like why he would stand with a particular person on a podium or make a statement in Russia that was thought to be politically naïve. I would say, Give the guy a break! Billy Graham was called by God to be an evangelist, to preach the Gospel. Let's honor a servant of the Lord who's preached the Gospel. He's not done it angrily or polemically; he's done it by lifting up Christ. He has never dishonored Christ by any fiscal or moral or mean-spirited scandals. So let's give him credit, let's give him some space; he's been faithful. When people persist in being critical, I say, "OK, here's the last thing I am going to state: all the women in my life—my mother, my wife, my sisters—came to Christ through Billy Graham."

Gerald Beavan   There were some who were fundamentalists doctrinally and others who were fighting fundamentalists. Fundamentalism didn't become a very gentle expression of the Christian faith. We're told in the Scripture to contend for the faith. I used to say they became contentious for the faith. Billy saw that they were more wrapped up in little petty points of doctrine or interpretation but weren't really fulfilling the Great Commission, which is to preach the Gospel to every creature. He had to gradually distance himself from those people who, in the language of the Scripture, were straining at a gnat and swallowing a camel. Billy just felt that fighting over some of those issues was not his calling—that preaching the Gospel *was*. As far as the fundamentals of the faith, Billy never shed even one of them.

Ben Armstrong   The opposition from the right was more difficult for Billy to accept; he expected it from the left. The people from the right had supported him earlier in his ministry. They were upset by what they cited as his compromising position in referring converts to various groups that didn't share his primary concern about evangelism. They also were upset by Billy's accepting on the platform people who did not agree with him all the way theologically.

William Martin   Where he has protected himself was years ago, putting himself under the control of a real board made up of people of substance and accomplishment. So if they told him, This is not a good idea, he was inclined to listen to them.

Why Do People Respond to Evangelism?

Paul Ferrin   The easy answer through the years has been guilt, fear. But beyond that there is the attraction of being caught up with the emotion of many people—the need for self-help accompanied with [being with] other people, a searching for something they didn't [have] in their ordinary, day-to-day experiences. Basically people are still afraid of God. Evangelism is a way to hit that button.

Why Do People Respond to Billy Graham's Form of Evangelism?

Robert J. Johannson   Different people have had discussions as to how to explain his success. Some say it is his integrity, which I am certain is top notch. Some say it's the staff he has gathered around him—he's got George Beverly Shea, who is still singing in his nineties. This is wonderful. But many people have good singers; many people have integrity. What I saw is that if there is anything the Father is doing, he is reconciling the world to himself, through his son Jesus. The whole idea of Calvary is God's love for a lost world. So if God is doing anything, it's redemptive. That's what Jesus did, and that's what Graham did. The secret of his success is that he was doing what God was doing. And he had the ability to stay focused. I do believe that Graham was doing what the Father was doing, that is, telling the world that God loves them. That is the basis of his success.

Maurice Rowlandson   I've always said that one of Billy Graham's strengths was that he got hooked on preaching the Gospel and didn't get sidetracked on other things. Even when it came to the time toward the end of his ministry, and [they] started working to get food to help the local needy, he left it to his colleagues.

Gerald Beavan   I used to say when people asked why people responded to Billy's messages that Billy could stand up and say poodily doo for twenty minutes, give an invitation, and have souls. His great gift was giving the invitation—bringing people to their decisions for Christ. If you have heard Billy ten times, you probably have heard all of his sermons. They may have a slightly different text, and a slightly different introduction, but essentially they're all the same. He never went empty at the invitation. The gift of the spirit that was given to him was to give the invitation.

Billy Kim   So many people were touched by the Seoul Crusade. In one instance, a high school boy was walking on the river bank when he saw this crowd of people. So he came out of curiosity, got converted, went on to seminary, was ordained, and went to Mongolia, where he established a university. A few years ago I asked this man to write his personal testimony. He did, and I sent it to Ruth Graham. She told me, "This is what Billy needs, to encourage his heart."

Leighton Ford   I believe the crusades Billy had across the years were very significant, not only because of the individuals touched but what they would bring to a city of religious reality, with the churches working together. A Billy Graham crusade was not only evangelistic in the sense of reaching out to new Christians; it was also an umbrella and time of celebration for a family coming together. I think that's missing today, and I don't know what will replace it.

When Billy first came on the scene after World War II, he was reaching many people in cities, people who had moved from the South to the Midwest or the West Coast, and the crusades recalled their roots. When the society became more pluralistic, with many more niches, it became more difficult for anything to make an impact upon a large group of people, so we have had to go to other ways of evangelism. I believe local church evangelism has become more important. I think a good deal of what happened in Youth for Christ and in the Graham rallies is now taking place through the megachurches, what Peter Drucker called the "pastoral churches."

Michael Deaver   I first met Billy Graham in the late 1960s, when he came to Governor Reagan's office in Sacramento. I had seen him as a college student during his crusade in San Jose but I had not been up close. When I did meet him, I found him to be an impressive figure.

Leighton Ford   I had become the president of a youth group in my hometown in Canada, and I had met Billy in some conferences and had been very impressed with him. I remember his blue gabardine suits, his hand-painted ties, and his pointing finger, and how impressive he was as a speaker. He had been very gracious to me. In those early years, he asked me to sit in on a planning meeting and take the notes even though I was the youngest person there.

I'd say we have a mixed relationship; I wouldn't say we've been close, but it's been affectionate and appreciative on both of our parts. I'm a good bit younger than Billy, so I was not there at the level of age and experience, as were the Wilson brothers, and he was not a mentor in terms of spending a good deal of time with me. But he was certainly very strategic in encouraging me at various times in my life. He was very protective of me at times. When I began to preach in the late sixties with more of an emphasis on the social implications of the Gospel, I know some of the people around him were very critical. They thought I had abandoned the old-time Gospel, but Billy was always very supportive. Although I don't see him a great deal now, I feel closer to him than in the earlier years, when I was in awe of the guy—I was young, he was my hero, my model. While I have great admiration for him now, I don't feel the same sense of awe as when I was a younger man.

Dwight Chapin   The first time I met Billy Graham was in Portland, Oregon, in 1968, and my initial impression of him was of his *blue, blue* eyes.

Roger Palms   I first met him at a crusade in Atlanta [in 1973]. My impression of him was very positive. I don't know what he thought of me. I was told he wanted to see me and I put on a good suit, but we had some terrific thunderstorms and I got soaked. It turned out he couldn't see me that night. The next night, the same thing happened. The third night, I decided that if I was going to get all wet I would wear an old suit and scruffy shoes. It did rain, and I looked like a drowned rat when I finally met him.

I feel honored to have been able to work with Billy Graham. He never disappointed me. His faithfulness was an encouragement to me. I wanted to be a better writer, a better dad, and a better Christian because I worked with Billy Graham. He taught me in the prayer times and in Bible study times how to relate to people. I don't think I would have the ministry I still have—writing, teaching, and editing—if it hadn't been for what Billy Graham taught me. He has been a blessing in my life. I am a richer man for it.

Millie Dienert   He never changed. He had a burning desire which he constantly shared with his associates. They in turn felt the same desire. People wanted to work for him because the man was always the same, with the same heart's desire.

Joyce Mostrom   I attribute it to the Lord's doing. It was just a wonderful work of God to choose this man to do this wonderful work. I always felt that God has used him marvelously and that he has been given the grace to live with integrity. I have always looked up to him and honored him a great deal.

Louis Zamperini   He will be remembered as the greatest evangelist of all time, having reached more people in the world than any other evangelist; he has spoken to more people in the world than anybody. He will also be remembered as one of the few evangelists that led an impeccable life. He has been a true, faithful Christian all these years. He never failed anybody once. We look up to him as God's chosen evangelist. That's the way it is. We still correspond once a month.

Henry Holley   He knows who he is. But yet he doesn't go around talking about who he is. He has a pretty high standard for himself—the perception people have of him that he has to maintain. He'll never ride in a Cadillac; he'll never sit on the same seat in an automobile with a woman other than his wife or a member of the family; he'll never be in a hotel room with the door closed with a woman other than his wife. I have heard Billy say many times, "I will never bring discredit upon my Lord."

Michael Deaver   He will be remembered by Christian organizations as the twentieth century's greatest evangelist. I guess that's pretty good. There is a huge surge in fundamentalism, in Christianity and in Islam. When I grew up, the church in this country was left. To call the National Council of Churches, the World Council of Churches, the heads of every mainstream church "liberal" was to be kind. Now everybody, all of a sudden, is worried about the Christian right. But in my view, Billy Graham never urged people to go out and work in school board elections or get involved in politics. His only message was, Get yourself right with your Savior.

Charles Riggs   The Holy Spirit was really active in Billy's heart because Billy loved the Lord and wanted to please Him in everything he did. Billy was in the ministry just to preach Christ; he was not looking to be heralded or thought of as some kind of big shot. I believe that was the secret of Billy's life.

As Graham's ministry grew in the post–World War II period, his fame increased, and he became the major spokesman for evangelical Protestantism. Having been influenced previously by his father-in-law, Nelson Bell, as well as by the scholarly evangelicals Carl F. H. Henry, Harold Lindsell, and Harold John Ockenga, Billy now sought to balance his social conscience with the classic fundamentals of orthodox faith.

Although Ockenga, who held an earned doctorate and served as pastor of Boston's historic Park Street Church, acknowledged that the doctrinal positions of fundamentalism and neoevangelicalism—the latter being the movement championed by Billy and his associates—were identical, he contended that fundamentalism had no interest in, or mechanism to deal with, the challenging societal problems of the post–World War II world. As Ockenga wrote: "The new evangelicalism embraces the full orthodoxy of fundamentalism, but maintains a social consciousness and responsibility which was strangely absent from fundamentalism. The new evangelicalism concerns itself not only with personal salvation, doctrinal truth and an eternal point of reference, but also with the problems of race, of war, of class struggle, of liquor control, of juvenile delinquency, of immorality, and of national imperialism. . . . The new evangelicalism believes that orthodox Christians cannot abdicate their responsibility in the social scene."

Subscribing to the new evangelicalism, Billy placed the highest priority on personal salvation—first because all people must be reconciled to God, and second because he believed the radical transformation that occurs in the life of the born-again will lead inexorably to development of social concern. In 1965, commenting on the problems of race and war in his book *World Aflame,* he wrote: "I say that these and all other problems can be solved, but only at the Cross. The cross of Christ is not only the basis of our peace and hope; but it is also the means of our eternal salvation. The object of the cross is not only a full and free pardon; it is also a changed life, lived in fellowship with God. This is the message for the world today. This is the message of hope and peace and brotherhood."

———————

Gerald Strober   Billy expounded on that theme in response to questions posed by me and my coauthor, Lowell Streiker, in the preparation of our book *Religion and the New Majority,* that "it is the very nature of Christian concern that we become aware of social needs and wherever possible do all that can be done to alleviate the suffering of humanity. This is a matter of Christian principle."

———————

In attempting to strike a balance between preaching the Gospel and expressing social concern, however, Graham would experience a certain tension, as was evident in his writing in *Christianity Today* that "we as Christians have two responsibilities; first to proclaim the Gospel of Jesus Christ as the only answer to man's deepest needs; and second, to apply as best we can the principles of Christianity to the social conditions around us."

In formulating his thoughts on social involvement, Billy was aware of sentiments expressed by one of his mentors, Carl Henry. Writing in *Christianity Today* in 1965 on the subject "Evangelicals in the Social Struggle," Henry suggested that the only meaningful manifestations of social reform that occurred in the last century resulted from the actions of evangelicals. Henry also concluded that the *ultimate* act of humanitarianism is the witness to salvation in Christ given by a Christian to a non-Christian.

Regarding the subject of improvement of relations among the races, Graham has certainly been a moderating force. His insistence, as far back as the 1950s, on integrated audiences at crusades was a major factor in breaking down perceived and actual barriers. He went further, integrating his staff by bringing the gifted evangelists Howard Jones, Ralph Bell, and Norman Sanders to the BGEA and by giving each man important assignments.

As Graham became more tolerant of racial, ethnic, and religious diversity—he delivered powerful messages to his core constituency by his inclusion of Roman Catholics in crusade planning and implementation and was outspoken in his opposition to anti-Semitism—people throughout the United States became less bigoted. If *Billy Graham*, who had come of age in the segregated South, could embrace African Americans, Catholics, Jews, and other minorities, those who had come forward at his meetings would follow his example.

His inclusion of Roman Catholics in his crusades is one of the most controversial aspects of his ministry. Over the years, many of his evangelical critics—and even some supporters—have attacked him for being soft on Catholic theology.

He grew up in an area where anti-Catholic sentiment was commonplace. At Bob Jones College, the Florida Bible Institute, and even at the relatively theologically enlightened Wheaton College, Roman Catholic doctrine and practice were viewed as inimical to historic Christian faith. Indeed, most evangelicals regarded Roman Catholics as being in need of personal salvation. So intense was the enmity between the two groups that in 1957 the Chicago-based Moody Bible Institute, then evangelicalism's leading center for Bible instruction, refused to lower its flag to half-staff following a fire in which many students attending a Roman Catholic parochial school on the city's west side were killed.

As Graham described his evolving view of Roman Catholicism in 1991, in an interview with *Bookstore Journal*, "Another significant thing happened in the early 1950s in Boston. Cardinal [Richard] Cushing in his magazine, *The Pilot*, put 'Bravo Billy' on the front cover. That made news all over the country. He and I became close, wonderful friends. That was my first coming to grips with the whole Protestant/Catholic situation. I began to realize that there were Christians everywhere."

Graham was able to claim by 1997 that "when we hold a crusade in any city now, nearly all the Roman Catholic churches support it."

His relationships with Cardinal Cushing and Archbishop Fulton J. Sheen notwithstanding, his most important association with a Catholic prelate was his friendship with Pope John Paul II, with whom he met on at least three occasions and whom he described as "a bridge builder . . . who bases his work and message and vision on biblical principles."

In an interview with the Associated Press in 1999, Graham predicted that John Paul would come to be regarded as "the man of the twentieth century," adding that "I admire his courage, determination, intellectual abilities, and his understanding of Catholic, Protestant, and Orthodox differences, and his attempt for some form of reconciliation."

If he was referring to *theological* reconciliation, he was out of sync with the great majority of contemporary evangelicals. Many held John Paul in high esteem, but they were troubled by his very traditional views, particularly with regard to the veneration of the Virgin Mary. Vatican officials have in recent years engaged in theological dialogue with Anglican, Lutheran, and Greek and Russian Orthodox academicians and clergy, as well as with representatives of the Jewish community, but there has not been similar discussion with evangelicals.

Chapter Eight

JUST AS HE *IS*

AN AMERICAN ICON

As Graham's ministerial reputation grew—along with his becoming a symbol of fiscal honesty and personal integrity—he became a national icon, an indispensable resource called upon to offer prayers at inaugurations of presidents, as well as to preside at their funerals. Then, when national tragedy struck, he helped the American people as they attempted to deal with their grief and fear—in 1995, when he was asked to speak at the memorial service for the victims of the Oklahoma City bombing, and in 2001, at the service held at the National Cathedral in Washington, D.C., in the wake of the terrible attacks of September 11. It was not that anyone expected Billy Graham to say anything startlingly new or profound. Rather, by his very participation in those memorials, he reassured the nation and the world that the American Ship of State remained on course.

There have been many factors in play in establishing his iconic status—first and foremost that he remains true to his calling, never wavering from his belief that God called him to be not an educator, missionary, pastor, or scholar but an *evangelist*. Despite his having addressed more people than any other evangelist—or, for that matter, any politician—and observing more people coming to Christ thanks to his preaching than has any other religious personality in the two-thousand-year history of Christianity, he does not succumb to pride in his accomplishments. Witness his words in the introduction to our book about a day in his life: "As for me, I can claim no supernatural power of my own. There are many godly and talented men but God has chosen me in his sovereign right to proclaim the message of salvation through faith in his son, Jesus Christ. Now this is a humbling truth. Therefore I find myself in the position of John and Charles Wesley, who took as a guiding passage from the Psalms, 'Not unto us O Lord, not unto us but unto thy name give glory, for thy mercy and for thy truth's sake'" (Psalm 115:1).

Bill Brown He was under much pressure to undertake large projects, such as starting a college, but his heart was always in evangelism, and that's where he wanted it to be.

Gerald Beavan There was great pressure to have a Billy Graham university. I was among others who opposed that idea. I was also among others who opposed the idea of his going into politics. Billy's calling was to be an evangelist, and nothing else should have been allowed to interfere with that.

William Martin At one time the businessman H. R. Hunt asked Billy to run for political office. Billy discussed this with Ruth, and she said, "You won't have a chance because this country won't elect a divorced man."

Ruth's Role in His Success

William Martin She played quite a significant role with the children, and she played a role with him in providing him with an island of stability. From time to time she also played a role in calling his hand and serving as a foil to argue with him on things. A number of people have said that there would have been no Billy Graham without Ruth. She held his feet to the ground, and occasionally perhaps to the fire. I think as much as anything she has provided that core of stability. She played a very major role in keeping the family from going adrift so that that didn't become a shame on his ministry, as it had, for example, with people like Billy Sunday.

Ben Armstrong Ruth was a great help to him. What she brought to the table was not only a winsome personality and an excellent intelligence, but she also brought a cultural background that she received growing up as a missionary's daughter in China. She had experiences that helped Billy become an international personality.

Anna-Lisa Madeira   She is an adviser and gives him much of his illustrative sermon material.

Charles Massey   Ruth is a booster, a backer, a savant with him. He pays a great deal of attention to what she says. Billy needed her attitude toward what he was and what he was doing, and Ruth was a balance. She never sought the headlines; she didn't try to be a large personality like he was.

Bill Brown   Ruth is a very smart, very clever, deep Christian who has had much influence on Billy's life. When it came to the film ministry, he was very strong about Ruth's participation. If she felt that something was wrong, we really had to look at it very closely. Perhaps we haven't even been aware of all of her advice and help to him.

Gerald Beavan   Ruth has been the rudder for much of his life to keep him focused. She has been a very faithful prayer supporter. She is very plainspoken, and if Billy wanted to do something ridiculous she would say, "Oh, *come on*, Bill," and he wouldn't do it.

Billy Kim   On the final day of the Seoul Crusade, I met with Mr. Graham at 2:00 P.M. in his hotel room to go over his sermon. I noticed that Mrs. Graham was packing, and I asked her: "Do you do all his packing wherever he goes?" And she said: "Yes, that's not one of his gifts."

Gerald Beavan   He was not a particularly orderly, well-organized person; he was not systematic. One of the great experiences of life was to watch him repack his suitcase when we were finishing a crusade and were going to leave town: he would throw things into the suitcase from where they were all over the room. In Boston, before the meeting on Boston Common, we met in Billy's room for prayer. It was a cloudy, drizzly, typical New England day, and right in the middle of his prayer Billy said, "Oh Lord, where's my hat? I can't find my hat." And he kept on praying. Maybe thirty seconds later he said, "Oh here it is," and kept on praying.

And Billy was not a particularly good businessman. Ruth used to say that every now and then she'd get a call from their banker in North

Carolina and as soon as he would identify himself, she'd say, "How much has he overdrawn *now?*" Billy would be generous to a fault and write checks when there wasn't money to cover them in their personal account. One day, we were walking near the Mayflower Hotel in Washington, and a street person asked him for money. Billy gave him a few dollars, and I rebuked him saying, "Bill, he's just going to use that to buy booze." I have never forgotten his reply. He said, "What he does with it is *his* responsibility; my responsibility is to be kind to people in need." I think that was almost a rule of life for him.

Billy Kim   When the Grahams arrived in Seoul, we met them at the airport and I rode with them to their hotel. At one point, Mrs. Graham asked me how many children I had and their names. I told her I had three children and that their names were Joey, Mary Kay, and John. The next day, Ruth Graham asked me: "How's Joey, how's Mary Kay, how's John?" It really touched me that she remembered their names and asked me how they were doing.

Arthur Bailey   She has always been a very feisty, high-spirited person. In the late spring of 2005, I went to see Billy at his home. He said, "Say hello to Ruth." I thought she looked exceptionally well and told her so. She replied, "Oh, stop lying!"

Leighton Ford   She is a delightful person and I have great admiration for her. I went to see her last spring. She was in her big chair, not able to move. She cannot see to read unless she has a large screen where she has the Psalms in very large letters. She has memorized Psalm 119, the longest chapter in the Bible.

I said, "Ruth, how are you?" She said, "Fine." I said, "How are you, *really?*" She replied, "Fine." I said, "Define 'fine.'" She answered, "I am as content as a mouse on a glue pad." I said, "What is *that?*" Ruth replied, "It's a thing you catch mice on." I asked, "How do you know the mouse is content?" She said, "Have you ever heard one *complain?*" That little incident speaks for Ruth. She is uncomplaining. She's gone through a lot: growing up in a difficult place in China, Billy being gone all those years, the struggles the children have had, and yet she doesn't complain. She is a very gifted poet with a deep appreciation for literature. She and Billy are, in a way, very different people. But certainly, although it has not always been easy they have had a wonderful romance all these years. Right now, Billy can hardly hear anything and Ruth can only talk very weakly, so it is very difficult for them to communicate, and so they look at each other and hold hands, which is very poignant right now.

His Attributes

Blessed with a strong profile; impressive mane of hair; tall stature; and a powerful, southern-accented speaking voice, whether entering someone's living room or Yankee Stadium Graham would immediately command the attention of all present. He possessed not only charisma (well before that now-too-often-used term was widely in use) but the ability to concentrate on the person, or multitude, to whom he was speaking.

He also possessed a capacity for hard work—not that he didn't enjoy vacations, or walks in the mountains near Montreat—and he was always aware of the enormous responsibilities of his ministry. When he was not on the road, his days were filled with staff meetings, telephone calls, answering the mail, and conferring privately with a range of people, but also with Bible study, prayer, and preparation of sermons.

He had the capacity to preach *every* night for weeks on end; witness the Harringay and Madison Square Garden Crusades. It may be difficult for one to comprehend what enormous reserves of stamina have been required of Billy Graham over the many years of his ministry in fulfillment of his varied commitments, as well as the emotional strength and control he has had to summon day after day, month after month, to be able to stand before thousands of people and speak to them of their eternal destiny. Through it all, for more than sixty years, Billy Graham has had the responsibility of being *Billy Graham*.

He is, of course, not without flaws. An inveterate name-dropper, he has over the years embellished his sermons with references to the high and mighty. In terms of oratory, he is far from being the world's greatest preacher; witness his often rambling and at times downright dull sermons. Yet people respond.

He had the good fortune of coming to prominence during the era of advances in communications and transportation. "The Hour of Decision" radio program brought him a huge audience, but with the advent of television, and with the viewer being able to observe him close up, his impact extended far beyond the boundaries of his crusades. With the introduction of jet aircraft, he and his team were able to cross the world in a matter of hours, rather than days.

Leighton Ford   I was asked at Duke Divinity School (at the time when *Christian Century* was carrying a series of articles on "How My Mind Has

Changed") how Billy had changed over the years I had been with him. A picture came to my mind of an arrowhead, and I said, "I think Billy Graham has been like an arrowhead. He's kept that sharp cutting edge of his message like the point of an arrow; wherever he goes it's that simple message of John 3:16, that God so loved the world that he gave his Son. But then, like the base of an arrow, he's grown in his understanding of the implications of that Gospel; whether it be for race relations or concern for poverty or nuclear war."

I believe that is very significant because many leaders as they get older get flatter—they develop many interests, but they lose that sharp cutting edge—and others get narrower; it's like plucking one string all the time. Billy has had the unusual ability to keep that very clear, sharp focus and to grow and understand the implications of that Gospel. And like the shaft of an arrow to go deeper, maybe in a way gentler and mellower, in understanding his shortcomings and the shortcomings of other people.

Billy Graham Today

Arthur Bailey   It is an oxymoron, but Billy is at his weakest point in life yet he is at his strongest point in terms of influence. So while he is at his weakest point physically, he has greater influence today than ever before.

Gerald Beavan   I was in a restaurant two or three months ago and asked the waitress where she was from. She had an accent, and I said, "I was once in your country." She asked why I had been there and I said I had worked with Billy Graham. And she said, "Who?" I said, "Billy Graham." And she said, "Who is *that*?" I think that people forget so quickly. Today Billy Graham's name is well known, but less well known than it was a year ago. Who knows anything about Billy Sunday or D. L. Moody today? I remember that when we were in Northfield in 1950, Billy and I went out to visit Moody's grave in this quiet little spot. We had a prayer, and some of the girls who were attending the school came by and asked us why we were standing there. We said, "We are here at Mr. Moody's grave." And one of the girls said, "*Who?*" And he [Moody] had founded the school that they were attending.

Leighton Ford   There are young people today who are not familiar with what he did thirty or forty years ago. There is a sense that he is a good man, sort of in the manner that people regard the pope. When Billy held his last crusade in Charlotte, the day before he started preaching I was working out in a gym next to the stadium and I heard two managers talking about the crowds that were expected. One of the managers asked the other, "Who *is* this Billy Graham guy, anyway?" The other replied, "He is an old fellow; he's older than Strom Thurmond" [the late senator from South Carolina, who retired in 2002 after more than a half-century of service and died on June 26, 2003, at age one hundred]. The first manager said, "What's he about, anyway?" And his colleague replied, "He just wants everybody to be *good*." I think there is this sense that Billy is a good, honest, loving, influential man who has done a lot of good and wants everybody to know God. In years to come, as his place in the history of religious life in America and the world is evaluated, he will certainly be regarded as one of the great evangelists of all time.

Anna-Lisa Madeira   I never wanted to take advantage of the fact that I had known him *when*. Of course, we kept in touch at Christmas time and still do. When Billy was in Providence in 1982, we were supposed to meet him at a luncheon but couldn't because of a previous commitment. We were quite disappointed. We went to the meeting in the evening. There, T. W. Wilson came up to us and told us that Billy wanted to see us. We had a lovely time together. He asked my husband, Dave, to pray for him, and then he called in his photographer to take a picture of the three of us. We had a personal note from him when our church, where my husband had been the pastor, had its fiftieth anniversary. We got their Christmas card the other day [it was December 2005] and he looks very tired—like a godly, Old Testament prophet. There is a certain beauty about the way he looks now.

Paul Ferrin   Billy Graham has mellowed. His worldwide experiences have become part of who he is in terms of a deep appreciation for God's work in ways other than what he may have expected when he was younger.

Ben Armstrong   He became more mature, if you can put it that way. In the years between 1966 and 1989, Billy was the keynote speaker at the annual conference of the National Religious Broadcasters many times, and I noticed that as time went on he tended to be more of a reasonable man and willing to talk about the issues with all kinds of people.

Charles Massey We were good friends and still are. And every time Billy is near here we have dinner together, or he comes to my house. When we go up to his house, it is like old home week. The thing I really like about Billy is that none of this went to his head. He is the same person that I knew almost seventy years ago. The Lord placed his hand on him and he was willing just to be *Billy Graham*. He didn't pontificate; he didn't become America's pope.

Lane Adams People ask me, What is Billy like? I answer, "What you see is what you get. You've seen him on television and heard him on radio; that's what he *is*—twenty-four hours a day." One person asked me a very perceptive question: "Have you ever seen him out of control, laughing?" I said, "Yes, on several occasions, when some team member made him the butt of a joke."

David Epstein One year [1992], Billy Graham was a guest on the Christmas special television program hosted by my sister, Kathy Lee Gifford. They were filming at Kathy's house in Greenwich, Connecticut, and she invited the family up. We spent the day with Mr. Graham and had a wonderful opportunity to be with him. When we broke for lunch, he asked if there was a McDonald's nearby because he wanted a quarter-pounder with cheese, and so we all had quarter-pounders with cheese.

Ben Armstrong He has a balance in his life that didn't follow the road of being elite and above the average person. He always seemed to keep his humility. He always remembered how he grew up and who he was despite the fame that he achieved.

Leighton Ford It's interesting about Billy that with his friends and family he is a bit of a name-dropper; he'll talk about the president he's been with, or whoever he's seen last. I never got the sense that he was bragging that he knew these people. It was rather the sense of, Ah shucks, what am I doing here?

Bill Brown His sense of proportion likely comes from the humility of his father and the dedicated Christian aspect of his mother. The greatest number of people probably would have given in to pride, but he seems to have kept that humility. He understood the position God had given him and was on his knees many times asking the Lord to reflect a life commensurate with that position.

Dwight Chapin   Billy Graham is so approachable, and I have very nice memories of him. His outgoing nature makes him special; he radiates love and has this incredibly deep belief that sustains him through illnesses.

Sidney Rittenberg   He is a man who has been listed among the ten greatest celebrities of the past twenty years or more, and yet he has remained essentially the same country preacher that he started out being in North Carolina. We have traveled to China three times with him and have been quite frequently in the Grahams' home. We have seen Billy in all sorts of circumstances of stress and contention. He is actually a very sincere, direct person; fame has never turned his head.

I am also impressed that this man, now well into his eighties, shows that rare ability to constantly continue to learn, to open new vistas, to examine his past activities, and to bring to light things that he considered mistakes and to learn from them and to go on. He is a very remarkable, very lovable person.

Charles Riggs   When Billy learned that my wife had died, Franklin was flying him in his airplane to the staff's annual meeting in West Virginia. Billy called me from the plane and invited me to attend.

Helen Stam Fesmire   Not long ago, a group of Charlotte citizens who are very proud of Billy wanted to honor him. He resisted, but finally said he would come. At the end of the meeting, Billy said, "Do you see the suit that I am wearing? It's new. My wife and children have told me that I have gotten rather slovenly in my old age. So I went out and bought this new suit for this occasion. It will be used one other time, and that is when I am buried in it."

Charles Massey   His sermons are as simple as they can possibly be. It's Jesus Christ as your savior; you need to repent, and God will save you. His life has been that simple. His home is simple; you would think he would live in a castle. He has never put himself forward. He had the commitment to do what he felt was the call of God, and he stuck to it. That's the secret of his life.

Millie Dienert   Anne is having a tremendous impact in her ministry, doing it *her* way. She is a very positive and eloquent speaker and does a wonderful job. I believe Anne's vision was really from her father. Anne's feeling—as is her father's—is, This is what God wants me to do that people will come to know God in a relative, rather than a theological, way—to know God in person and to know that He can live in your life.

Billy Kim   I have interpreted for many foreign preachers. Mr. Graham is the easiest one to interpret [for] because his sentences are so clear. In Seoul we both felt the Holy Spirit at work because people sensed there was only one voice coming out. Even today I meet people from all walks of life who were at the Crusade. I just held a crusade in Los Angeles with a large Korean congregation, and many of the people there told me they had either received Christ at Seoul or had dedicated to Christ at that meeting and are in the full-time ministry or otherwise serving the Lord.

William Martin   There is a complex mixture of ambition and humility, both of which are genuine. One of his long-time associates, Russ Busby, has observed that you have to have a big ego to get to be a big preacher. But Billy keeps his ego under control. The difference between Billy and some of the other preachers is that if God has something to say to him, at least He can get his attention. The people closest to him, Ruth, T. W. and Grady Wilson, would say, "You keep him faithful; we'll keep him humble." They loved him, but they weren't in awe of him.

Gerald Beavan   I never felt that Billy needs adulation from people. I think that his life, his ministry, and his achievements stand on their own—that they don't need to be embellished and almost glorified. Billy used to say that the real reason for his success is the people who had prayed for him. He said, "When we get to heaven, that little old lady who prayed for me every day has more to do with it than I did; I could only accomplish things because she prayed." He also used to say, like when he would be given the key to a city, "I'm going to lay this all at the Savior's feet; it's not for me, it's for *Him.*" I think he honestly felt that he really didn't deserve all the honors and recognition that he received—that he was doing his work in the service of his Lord.

David Epstein   [At the 2005 Crusade] he seemed the same wonderful man I had met in my sister's house thirteen years before. He was so humble, prayerful, compassionate, and filled with conviction about the Gospel, but not polemical. His spirit was still powerful, although he was obviously older and frailer.

Arthur Bailey   I believe that he will be remembered as someone who had an impact. He played so much more of a role than just as an evangelist; he became America's pastor. There is no one on the horizon today of that magnitude. He's a unique personality in history.

Dale Kietzman   He gave a big impetus to neo-evangelicalism because he was the most prominent spokesman. The other person I particularly associated with it, other than Carl [F. H.] Henry, was [Harold] Ockenga. He was fairly well known but only in church circles, not in the general public.

Bill Brown   One of my privileges was working for a man who was so respected by outsiders; people knew that he really wanted to represent the Lord the best he could. The fact that he was honest—that he had integrity—is what people will remember. I don't believe it will die off. I look at some of these old films of Billy at Wembley Stadium and at Madison Square Garden, and I wish every young person could see them.

Millie Dienert   The ministry will never be the same because it's minus the *he*. Let's face it, the crusades are called the Billy Graham Crusades and Billy Graham isn't there any more. But there will be an ongoing outreach to people because that is what evangelism is all about. It won't go on in the same manner as before because the personality is removed. But it can be a very effective ministry, and it's *going* to be. I know that Franklin has a heart for God; he doesn't want only [to] help the soul but *the body*. He puts both of them together.

The Question of Succession

In November 2000, William Franklin Graham III—known throughout his life as Franklin—was elected chief operating officer of the Billy Graham Evangelistic Association. Today, at age fifty-five, Franklin also serves as the BGEA's vice chairman and president.

Although Franklin made a decision for Christ at the age of ten, his teen and young adult years were marked by rebellious behavior. His smoking and drinking—decidedly not evidence of Fruits of the Spirit—gave Ruth and Billy many uneasy moments. Yet, aware of the pressures inherent in being Billy Graham's first-born son and namesake, they were patient, all the while praying that the Lord would straighten Franklin out.

One can imagine Ruth and Billy's relief and joy when in 1974, during a visit by Franklin to Israel, he was led by Roy Gustafson, a classmate of Graham's at the Florida Bible Institute and one of his long-time associates, to a genuine commitment to Christ.

Lane Adams   Franklin was a bad boy for a while. In recovering him out of one of his real bad periods—he was eighteen or nineteen years of age—Billy and Ruth sent him to work with two female missionaries who had a ministry to tubercular Bedouin in the northern Desert of Jordan. It was during that period when Franklin helped them build a hospital— he later served as chairman of the board of the hospital—that he had a complete turnaround.

Several years later, Franklin joined the staff of Samaritan's Purse, an evangelically oriented organization involved in relief efforts in the Third World. Then in 1979, following the death of Dr. Bob Pierce, its founder, Franklin became president of that organization, whose current annual budget exceeds $150 million.

Lane Adams   World Vision was founded by Bob Pierce, a man who combined a gigantic concern to relieve physical suffering and hunger with evangelistic zeal. We were having lunch at the Brown Derby restaurant in Hollywood (this was when he was in the terminal stages of leukemia) and he said to me, "Lane, I believe I have found my successor when I die." I said, "Who would that be?" He answered, "Franklin Graham." I said, "Bob, you're kidding; *no way.*" He said, "I have been taking him all over the world, and he really has a heart for the hurting people. I also find in him an evangelistic zeal." Franklin has justified Bob's faith in him.

Billy and Ruth's happiness over Franklin's changed life increased with his ordination on January 10, 1982, for the Gospel ministry, following the preaching of the sermon by his father. Seven years later, Franklin conducted the first of his own evangelistic events, called "festivals" rather than crusades.

Henry Holley   Now that Billy is not doing crusades anymore, I've been working with Franklin in helping him prepare his festivals. I don't know that any of us could step into our father's shoes. We could follow the fundamental principles, which never change, but *methods* change. Franklin is probably geared more to the society of his age group than Mr. Graham or I would be. That is reflected in the music and the style of programming. But I will say this: the message that Franklin preaches is the same as the message that Billy Graham preaches. I can close my eyes sometimes when Franklin is preaching and hear his father. I take great joy in the fact that Franklin is still proclaiming the same basic simple message.

Because Franklin grew up with the pressure of being Billy Graham's son, he must now experience the greater tension of being—at least in organizational terms—his father's successor. Without appearing to be macabre (and with the wish that Billy Graham lives to the biblical 120 years), when Graham does pass on, those pressures will most likely intensify.

In 2006 Franklin will hold festivals in five cities in the United States, as well as in Quito, Ecuador; and in Winnipeg, Canada. There is little doubt that he is an able administrator with a firm grasp of modern technology, a key element in maintaining the BGEA's status as one of the world's leading religious organizations.

The more important issue is whether Franklin will be able to attract large and enthusiastic crowds to his festivals. Will he succeed in filling stadiums, as did his father, who even in the twilight of his ministry set attendance records in Cincinnati, Dallas, and New York? Will Franklin be sought after by the world's leaders, whose friendship and confidence in Billy's counsel greatly contributed to his celebrity? Will Franklin, who in recent years has forthrightly spoken his mind on controversial issues, come to be viewed as divisive? With his father away from the public arena, will Franklin be able to capture and maintain the allegiance of tens of millions of evangelicals while gaining the high regard and affection shown Billy Graham over the years by the multitudes that exist outside the circle of evangelical faith?

Bill Brown   Before he had gotten into evangelism Franklin had proven himself on the social aspect, through Samaritan's Purse. He didn't just step into his father's shoes; he already had a complete, separate, functioning organization, and proved himself at it.

Charles Riggs   A few years ago, Franklin asked me to come to Dallas to train his men the way I did for Billy. When we prepared a crusade, we would be in a city for six months or longer, and we might have more than fifteen thousand people working with us, and Franklin wanted his people to learn the techniques we had used to draw large crowds. For two or three years, he has drawn audiences of up to fifty thousand.

Roger Palms   Franklin has four to six festivals, as he calls them, a year, so he is continuing the preaching ministry even as he has his Samaritan's Purse and Medical Missions ministry.

Maurice Rowlandson   There is some danger with Samaritan's Purse overshadowing the Gospel side of Franklin's ministry. People like to see things done; they don't always understand the faith aspect, and if they can do something they feel that means, in a sense, [that they are] earning their passport to heaven.

Gerald Beavan   I personally have admired Franklin for his forthrightness, for example in condemning Islam. He was not hesitant in criticizing President Clinton for his sexual fantasy there in the White House. Billy wouldn't have done either one of those things.

Helen Stam Fesmire   The things Franklin does, like helping hurricane victims, are not things that Billy would have done. But it is good that Franklin is using his abilities and energies in these ways. His crusades will likely be shorter; there won't ever again be weeks- or months-long meetings.

Stephen Linton   He is not like his father. He has a different perspective and a different agenda, and probably not as high a comfort level with that kind of high-profile interaction. He may not feel it as much to be a friend of the powerful. He's interested but he's not nearly as engaged as his father was, especially considering the relative status of their health. I wouldn't speculate on whether there is a more ideological bent to Franklin's view of North Korea than his father's. I believe that

Mr. Graham considered his visits to North Korea as part of his ministry—to be a friend of powerful people, to be someone that powerful people, as well as ordinary people, can turn to. He went out of his way to make himself available for that. Also, I believe he is comfortable with his role as a friend rather than as a mediator—as a big-picture person, rather than someone to negotiate details. I don't know that Franklin has come to the point in his ministry where he has a similar comfort level.

Gerald Strober   During the late 1990s, Jerry Falwell invited my wife, Deborah, and me to Lynchburg, Virginia, to attend commencement exercises at Liberty University. One of Franklin's sons was in the graduating class. Jerry had asked Billy to give the commencement address. The evening before the ceremonies, Jerry held a small reception at a local hotel. When Billy and Ruth arrived, Deborah and I sat with them for a few minutes, exchanging pleasantries. Then I noticed that Franklin was standing in the middle of the room, and we walked over and introduced ourselves. We could sense immediately that he had little interest in meeting us. As I mentioned that I had written a book on a day in the life of his father, I noticed that Franklin was already focusing on the next person waiting to greet him.

Charles Riggs   Franklin was kind of a cowboy—he was all over the place—and they were really worried about him. But it is wonderful how he turned out to be a real leader. He has preached all over the world to large crowds and has been well accepted. I understand that he may ask his dad to speak for one night at one of his festivals. He wants to make sure that Billy is not forgotten, and I am absolutely sure that Billy is confident in Franklin's ability to carry the ministry on. Franklin has really gotten down to business. He is a powerhouse himself now, and Billy is now sitting back and enjoying life.

Bill Brown   Franklin is a very independent young man. He has done a great job on the social aspects, and if he can do as well with the evangelistic aspects it's in good hands. He has very good people working with him who will probably come up with many unique ideas. As long as Billy is alive, that will help Franklin. Even though Billy doesn't have crusades, the respect and love is there enough that he'll ask people to support Franklin—and they *will*. It is difficult to know what will happen when the Lord takes Billy. Franklin is having very successful meetings; and since

Christians are always behind successful evangelistic efforts, perhaps he will get a similar amount of support.

Ben Armstrong Franklin is doing very well. We knew him because my son, Bob, was his classmate at Stony Brook School, on Long Island. We knew Franklin to be a young man with great energy, a person who had a problem with many of the strict rules of this prep school. But he had a lot of energy and a lot of the personality traits of his father. He was a good speaker. It's probably not fair to ask him to replace his father. He has made his own way, made his own decisions, made his own life, and has been very successful. He is buoyed up by that magic name of Graham.

David Epstein I love Franklin's combination of the truth and the humanitarian compassion ministry, which gives him a credential to build on his dad's ministry.

Gerald Beavan In 2003, Billy had a meeting in San Diego and he and I spent some time together. When we parted, we realized this was probably the last time we would be together. The team stayed in the largest hotel downtown. I was not present, but one of the team members told me that they were scheduled to have a prayer meeting every morning. On the first morning, there were about twenty-three of them sitting there in this room, chatting, and Franklin came in and stepped up to the platform and asked the person in charge of local arrangements, "How many rooms do we have here in this hotel?" That person answered, "Ninety-nine." Franklin then observed that there must be more than a hundred people in the group, and he said, "There are twenty-three people here. My father is not well. He is going to be preaching every night. You are going to be here every morning praying for him. This is not a request. This is an *order.*" And he left the room.

The next morning, everybody was there. Franklin has brought quite a bit of order and discipline into the operation. What impressed me about that story was the fact of ninety-nine rooms and that more than a hundred people were part of the crusade. In the old days, we held crusades in very large cities, but we never had more than fifteen people; we never had those huge entourages that became the rule in the later years. In the old days, we all used to wear two or three hats.

Arthur Bailey Franklin calls his meetings "festivals," which may be a way of separating himself from his father. But the meetings are essentially the same. After September 11, in response to Muslim sensitivities Billy called his meetings "missions," rather than crusades. Franklin was concerned that people would be confused; Would they assume that the word *mission* meant we were doing something different? So we went back to using *crusade* for Mr. Graham's meetings.

Maurice Rowlandson When Billy was preaching at his zenith, we used to get questions all the time in the London office as to who will replace him. God only knows. Franklin is a very good preacher and evangelist, but he hasn't got the same humility as his father. Billy Graham always put himself behind everybody else. He never wanted to take the prime position. But I don't think that is quite so true with Franklin.

Howard Jones Franklin is not Billy, but he's a fine man. He preaches a different message, and the Lord is honoring his meetings in different parts of the world. All of us on the team who are retired were happy to see that the anointing is on him. We need to pray for him.

Robert J. Johannson The most touching thing is Franklin's love for his father; he is very protective of him. It is a very beautiful thing when you understand Franklin's journey—the pain and embarrassment he probably caused Mom and Dad. God is great and full of grace and redemptive power.

Franklin has very strong social context to his ministry through Samaritan's Purse. For him to rise to his father's level as an evangelist is impossible. But maybe it's not necessary. Maybe evangelism in the future has to have a social content. Maybe that's what God is saying. It wasn't so in the fifties; I think the gospel of the fifties was in many ways devoid of social content. And that is to our chagrin. Maybe we are looking for another Billy Graham but God's plan is to weld the social gospel to redemption more than Dr. Graham did.

Gerald Beavan Today, if you measure things financially, Samaritan's Purse is larger than the BGEA. Franklin is already trimming down the BGEA's size, so the BGEA will either have to be with Franklin as the front man or it will merge with Samaritan's Purse. The potential for the two organizations becoming one is probably very real.

David Epstein In terms of looking down the road, you have to wonder if there is anyone we know now ministering that could be another Billy

Graham in the sense of mass crusade evangelism. More and more, mass evangelism is being done through technology—the Internet and television. Who knows what God will do? It may be the end of an era. I would be amazed if any one individual could attract such crowds again. But our God is great; he could certainly do that. He could raise up in a new way someone who is already on the scene. I'd be amazed if anyone emerged that would be in the role of Billy Graham. I have a feeling it's going to be more a leadership by committee.

Gerald Beavan   There was a time when Leighton Ford was assumed to be the heir apparent. I used to say that God's men are pulled up from above; they are not pushed up from beneath. Whether Franklin will become an international evangelist as Billy was, I just don't know; I don't believe anybody knows. Maybe there won't be another evangelist like Billy; maybe modern communications will change all that. I understand that Franklin is a very good preacher. He has not had as adequate theological training as I personally think he should have, but he certainly knows the word of God. And he certainly is a businessman and a good organizer.

Leighton Ford   They were wonderful years, and I am very grateful and thankful for the results of them that I still come across. I myself never thought there would be a successor to Billy. I suppose that Franklin is as close as there can be. It was never my particular ambition. I felt restlessness in my own spirit that I had been involved in crusade evangelism for thirty years. I was kind of tired of that, and I felt there was something more that I needed to do. I also sensed that there were changes taking place in the Billy Graham Association—that when Billy was through and his public ministry was over, there would have to be some shrinking of the organization. I had a long talk with Allen Emery, chairman of the BGEA executive committee, who said that the time had come when I should venture out on my own. It wasn't easy for me to accept this at that time. But looking back, it was a very realistic assessment and exactly the right thing to do.

It turned out that, at that same time, there were two other factors: one was the death of our son, Sandy, at the age of twenty-one, during heart surgery at Duke University. At that time, I had been approached by Gordon-Conwell Seminary to be their president. Fuller Seminary wanted me to teach evangelism, and other organizations had wanted me to work with them. My wife and I prayed about this, and we decided to put everything aside for a couple of years. It was during that time that our son died. Out of that loss there was a desire to help other men and women with their ministry. I had also noticed, as chairman of the Lausanne Committee, that a major leadership change was taking place worldwide, within the church and other organizations, that many of the leaders, like Billy and his peers, who had emerged after World War II, were coming to an end of their ministry and there was a whole new group under forty who were emerging with some new visions, but oftentimes without much mentoring. All of that led us to start something new. That is why we launched Leighton Ford Ministries, to focus on that next generation.

William Martin   I'm sure he [Billy Graham] feels he's fallen short; that's part of his nature and his theology. But he's also recognized what he's accomplished. He once said to me that there are a lot of young men around, but that realistically he didn't see anyone who would be able to accomplish what he had accomplished. He didn't mean, Nobody is as good as I am [or that] God hasn't touched anybody else. He meant that the situation has changed in the sense that no one person is likely to predominate.

Henry Holley   The average person will probably expect that this is a dynasty, that Franklin will be like his father. But Franklin is his own man. As far as attendance is concerned, anyone who looks at it should ask, What did Billy Graham do when *he* was fifty-three years old? What kind of crowds did *he* have? If you make that kind of comparison with Franklin, it would likely be about the same. Of course, it is human nature to ask whether Franklin will measure up to his father. That is certainly not Franklin's goal. He wants to be faithful to the calling that God has put on his life; he is his own man. He is gifted in many ways. He has the passion for evangelism of his father and the compassion for the hurting people from his Momma. That is a good balance, both for evangelism and for social activity.

Leighton Ford   I don't think anyone can step into another's shoes; God has made us all unique people. Billy is very unusual in all ways and, I believe, has had a singular call to this ministry. Franklin is his own person.

He has some of Billy's attributes and some that Billy *didn't* have. We have to take him for what he is.

Roger Palms Remember, Billy Graham didn't start out to be *Billy Graham*. God the Holy Spirit took that faithfulness of his and kept expanding it. God used Billy's brilliance and skills and humility and expanded that into a worldwide mission. Nobody's going to be the next Billy Graham. There's only *one*. Franklin is his own man, and he does things *his* way—he preaches *his* way—and that's very wise.

AFTERWORD

In examining Billy Graham's life, the what-ifs of history are especially intriguing. What if he had remained at Bob Jones College? What if he had decided that the education he received at Florida Bible Institute was fully adequate in preparing him for ministry? What if Ruth Bell had not chosen him as her life's partner? What if he had not contracted the mumps and thus had been able to join the military chaplaincy? What if he had refused Torrey Johnson's offer to work for Youth for Christ and taken a pulpit? What if Hearst had not directed his editors to "puff Graham"? What if Bev Shea had remained at WMBI and Cliff Barrows had continued his ministry with his wife Billie? What if Graham had not met, and respected, the advocates of the new evangelicalism? What if Harringay had been a dismal failure or Graham had been vanquished at the Garden? What if he had lacked both the stamina and emotional stability to travel the world, preaching the Gospel? What if there had been an earlier onset of the illnesses and physical infirmities that debilitated him in later life? What if, along the way, he had lost his vision, humility, and sense of proportion? What if he had entered politics or established a college or theological seminary or accepted any one of the many attractive and lucrative offers outside of the field of evangelism?

Given his early training at home, his conversion as a teenager, and his dedication to the Lord, Graham would likely have been successful in any form of full-time Christian service. Had he not become an evangelist, however, how would millions throughout the world, drawn by the power of his celebrity to his crusades and meetings, have found faith in Christ? How would the lives of those multitudes have been influenced had they not been able to hear him on the radio or see him in films and on television, or—surrounded by thousands of other spiritually needy souls—be caught up in the drama of one or more of his many crusade services?

There have been among his contemporaries other gifted evangelists and preachers, some more eloquent than he, but it is unlikely that any one of them would have been capable of drawing huge numbers of people to their meetings. Nor would they have earned the national and international renown that enabled Billy to demonstrate that mass evangelism—in the right hands—could be a respectable form of Christian witness.

Given the ephemeral nature of celebrity, as well as the likelihood that his organization will in time fade in influence, it may be that he will not be remembered beyond one or two generations—especially as people are drawn to new heroes and seek meaning in faiths other than orthodox Christianity.

Yet Billy Graham's influence is impressive. In his single-minded devotion to soul winning and in his ability to create and maintain an organization focused on propagating the Gospel, he has succeeded by bringing large numbers of individuals into the Christian fold, providing the critical mass of the contemporary religious right. Further, largely through his influence, American society—perhaps more now than previously in history—has come to reflect the values of evangelical Christianity. Thus it becomes difficult to imagine what American life would be like today had Graham not chosen and traveled on the evangelistic road.

As Graham descended the platform at Corona Park in the early evening hours of June 26, 2005, his final crusade recorded in the annals of history, he could rightly believe that he had in his more than eight decades on earth earned the encomium, "Well done, thy good and faithful servant."

Then, as he departed for the airport and the flight that would take him home at last, his mind was still fixed on the prize, his soul open to God's direction. The race he began in that tent in Charlotte so many years earlier had not quite run its course. In the words of Paul's letter to the Corinthians, he would for a time still see through the darkened glass, but surely, soon, Billy Graham would finally "See, and know, face to face."

THE AUTHORS

Deborah Hart Strober and Gerald S. Strober have collaborated on oral histories of the Kennedy, Nixon, and Reagan presidencies, as well as on oral biographies of Queen Elizabeth II and the Dalai Lama. Their oral biography of Rudolph Giuliani will be published in January 2007 by John Wiley & Sons. The Strobers, who recently celebrated their twenty-fifth wedding anniversary, live in New York City.

INDEX